Appetizers

Southern

Style

Recipes by:
The Junior League of
Greensboro, North Carolina

This book first published under the name
of *Out of Our League, Two*

Additional copies may be obtained from

Appetizers *Southern Style*
P.O. Box 117
Waycross, Ga. 31502

Revised edition
1st printing 1995, 10,000 copies
2nd printing 1997, 10,000 copies

ISBN: 0-94162-11-7

Printed by

FATHER&SON
PUBLISHING, INC.
4909 N. Monroe Street
Tallahassee, Florida 32303

TABLE OF CONTENTS

RECIPE AND IDEA CONTRIBUTORS

Clare Abel
Tena Anton
Carol Aplington
Kirt Austin
Mary Austin
Nancy Bain
Eloise Bell
Margaret Benjamin
Pat Bennett
Lynn Black
Lynne Blackmon
Melissa Block
Ginny Bogan
Meg Boyles
Beth Bramhall
Betty Braxton
Beth Brewer
Frances Bullock
Ann Carroll Burwell
Dale Caldwell
Sandra Canipe
Anne Carlson
Molly Carrison
Agnes Carstarphen
Millie Chalk
Judy Clement
Kathy Clendenin
Lynda Clifford
Kim Cochrane
Sally Cone
Betty Cone
Mary Cook
Terri Cooke
Jean Cornwell
Pat Cross
Bebe Crutchfield
Sallie Cunningham
Ann Davis
Carol Davis
Betsy Dawson
Ann Ditto
Sherry Donato
Ellen Drake
Mary Echols
Deanne Edwards
Jeanne Edwards
Pam Finn
Margaret Frassineti
Rachel Frick

Brenda Funderburk
Lee Gallien
Joe Gelzer
Jane Gibson
Marilyn Gideon
Margel Graham
Ginger Griffin
Beth Griswold
Kay Hagan
Ann Hageseth
Barbara Hall
Alfred Hamilton
Susan Hamilton
Louann Harlow
Beth Harrington
Betsy Harrington
Lane Harris
Cameron Harris
Ellen Henschen
Mabs Hicks
Betsy Hinerman
Cherie Holderness
Julie Holderness
Ann Holleman
Karen Hopper
Susan Howard
Gail Huggins
Dana Hunt
Karen Isner
Fran Jameson
Millie Johnson
Paula Johnson
Marcia Johnston
Babs Jones
Olive Jordan
Martha Kaley
Von Kimbrough
Joanie King
Jane Kirkpatrick
Mary James Lawrence
Brenda Lawson
Linda Lee
Ginni Lineberry
Mary Livingston
Sara Looman
Kay Maddox
Sherry Marus
Kim Mays
Martha McCormick

Beverly McCracken
Judy McGinn
Marie McLean
Karen McNeil
Kay McVey
Cynthi Metts
Julie Middleton
Spence Miller
Nancy Moore
Beth Morgan
Cotten Moring
Linda Mortenson
Leigh Murphy
Martha Neill
Cathy New
Judy Newlin
Bruce Nolan
Betsy Oakley
Donna Osswald
Fran Oxner
Mopsy Patterson
Martha Peete
Jackie Peoples
Gail Peterson
Anita Phipps
Betty K. Phipps
Holly Pierce
Laura Pierce
Suzanne Plihcik
Barbara Pomer
Helen Pope
Julie Powell
Alice Preyer
Judy Proctor
Susan Ridenhour
Chris Robinson
Millie Ronemus
Susan Ross
Mary Susan Ross
Camilla Ruffin
Sara Lee Saperstein

Dot Scott
Jessie Sellars
Betsy Shook
Dianne Shope
Jean Smith
Janet Sneed
Pam Sprinkle
Anne Sprock
Margaret Stauffer
Robin Moore Stiles
Susan Storrs
Janet Stout
Amelia Stout
Angie Stratton
Lynne Stroud
Martha Stukes
Mary Lillie Talton
Melissa Tankersley
Priscilla Taylor
Anne Taylor
Carol Taylor
Mary Thacker
Nicka Thornton
Suzanne Tilley
Pat Topolka
Cathy Valentin
Ann Wagg
Margaret Weatherly
Judy Wein
Gay White
Frann White
Judy White
Judy Wicker
Vickie Wilkins
Suzanne Williams
Katy Williamson
Jackie Wilson
Sally Winslow
Melinda Wood
Lauren Worth
Lynn Yancey

RECIPES

M·E·A·T

Saucy Tenderloin

Can partially do ahead

Serves: 10-12
Preparing: 30 min
Baking: 15-25 min

1	4-lb whole beef tenderloin, trimmed	1	7-oz can mushroom buttons, undrained
	several strips bacon	1	loaf French Bread, 2-inch diameter
1	5-oz bottle A-1 Sauce		
¼	lb butter		

Preheat oven to 400°. Lay several strips of bacon over the tenderloin. Place on rack in roasting pan and bake uncovered for 15 to 25 minutes total time (15 minutes for rare to 25 minutes for well done). While meat is cooking, heat A-1 sauce, butter, mushrooms and juice to boiling. Cut bread into small sandwich slices.

Slice meat into very thin pieces. Place meat on serving platter, spoon sauce over meat. Have bread on a separate tray. Place piece of meat on bread and eat as small open-faced sandwich.

Tenderloin Cubes
with Béarnaise Sauce

Can do ahead

Preparing: 10 min
Baking: 2-2½ hrs

**Beef tenderloin; any size,
    trimmed or untrimmed**

Preheat oven to 500°. Prepare tenderloin by folding tapered end under and securing with string for more uniform cooking. Do not salt or season. Place tenderloin uncovered in large roasting pan in oven.

To cook medium rare: bake 5 minutes per lb, if over 5 lbs
                                    bake 4 minutes per lb, if under 5 lbs

Turn off oven and let sit 1½ hrs. Do not open oven. After beef cools, cut into cubes.

Béarnaise Sauce

Can do ahead

Yield: 3 cups
Cooking: 20-30 min

½   **cup dry white wine**
4   **Tb tarragon vinegar**
2   **tsp dried tarragon**
½   **tsp freshly ground pepper**

8   **egg yolks, room
     temperature**
4   **Tb lemon juice**
½   **tsp hot sauce**
2   **cups butter, melted and hot**

In a small saucepan, combine wine, vinegar, tarragon and pepper. Bring to a boil and reduce to ¼ cup. Meanwhile, in the food processor with steel blade in place, combine egg yolks, lemon juice and hot sauce. Process 15 seconds. With machine running, in a steady stream add hot butter and then the reduced mixture. Cover and refrigerate if desired. Bring to room temperature before serving. *Can be used for sandwich spread or topping for vegetables such as broccoli and cauliflower.*

Marinated Beef

Must do ahead

1   cup sour cream
1½ tsp Dijon mustard
2   Tb lemon juice, divided
1   small clove garlic, crushed

salt and white pepper to taste
1   lb rare top sirloin, cut
      julienne
1   small onion, grated

Garnish

red tipped lettuce
watercress

fresh basil
lemon

Combine sour cream, mustard, 1 Tb lemon juice, garlic and pepper for marinade. In a large bowl, place the sirloin, onion and other 1 Tb lemon juice. Add marinade. Cover and refrigerate for several hours. Line a platter with red tipped lettuce, mound beef mixture, garnish with watercress, fresh basil and lemon twists. Serve with party picks.

Carpaccio

Must do ahead

Serves: 20
Preparing: 20 min
Cooking: 5 min

1	large onion	1	Tb parsley, chopped
¼	cup celery		freshly ground pepper
3	cloves garlic		salt to taste
⅓	cup olive oil	2	lbs raw beef tenderloin,
1¼	cups dry red wine		trimmed and sliced paper
1½	cups strong beef stock		thin

Combine onion, celery and garlic in food processor and chop very fine. Sauté in olive oil until golden. Add wine and beef stock. Cook over high heat for 5 minutes. Add parsley, pepper and salt. Spoon some hot liquid into a deep 2-quart casserole. Add single layer of beef. Continue to add layers of liquid and beef until all is used up. Cover and refrigerate 24 to 48 hours, but no longer. To serve, drain and arrange beef on platter and cover with freshly chopped parsley, or roll a slice of beef, skewer with a wooden pick and dip in chopped parsley.

Partially frozen meat is easier to slice paper thin. If thawed, partial freezing time for slicing:

1½-inch thick meat	1½ hours
1-inch thick meat	1-1¼ hours

If frozen, partial thawing time for slicing:

- at room temperature:

1½-inch thick meat	1¼ hours
1-inch thick meat	45 minutes

- in microwave (full power):

¾ lb. meat	55 seconds

Sour Dough Beef Dip

Serve immediately

Yield: 2½ cups
Preparing: 20 min
Baking: 1½ hrs

1 **8-oz pkg cream cheese, softened**	**dash of Worcestershire sauce**
1 **cup sour cream**	2 **Tb green pepper, finely chopped**
1 **4-oz pkg chipped beef, shredded**	1 **8-inch round loaf sour dough bread**
¼ **cup green onion, finely chopped**	

11:00   12:30   done

Thoroughly combine all ingredients except bread. Slice top off bread round and hollow out carefully, making sure there are no weak places in bread shell. Fill the shell with beef dip and put top back on. Wrap in foil and bake at 300° for 1½ hours. Cube bread taken from interior of loaf and serve around baked loaf to dip in hot mixture.

Barbecups

Can do ahead
Can freeze

Yield: 12 or 36
Preparing: 30 min
Baking: 12 min

1 **lb ground beef**	1 **10-count can buttermilk flaky biscuits**
½ **cup bottled barbecue sauce**	¾ **cup cheddar cheese, grated**
1 **Tb instant minced onion**	
2 **Tb brown sugar**	

Brown beef and drain. Add barbecue sauce, onion and brown sugar. Set aside. Separate biscuit dough into 12 biscuits and press each one into bottom and sides of a greased muffin cup. May cut each biscuit into thirds and use 36 minature muffin cups. Spoon mixture into cups. Sprinkle with cheese. Bake at 375° for about 12 minutes or until golden brown.

Appetizer Empanadas

Can do ahead
Can freeze

Yield: 40
Preparing: 30 min
Baking: 20 min

1	lb lean ground beef	1	tsp garlic powder
½	cup onion, minced	1	tsp coriander
6	Tb red chili salsa, hot or mild		salt and pepper to taste
2	tsp chili powder	1	10-oz pkg frozen patty shells, thawed
1	tsp cumin		

Beef filling: Sauté crumbled beef and onion in skillet until beef is cooked and onion is soft. Drain. Stir in remaining ingredients except patty shells. Set aside.

Place thawed patty shell dough on a floured board. Roll out in 1 piece to about ⅛ inch thick. Cut dough into 3 inch rounds. Spoon 2 tsp of filling on each dough circle. Fold each over into half circle. Moisten edges with water and press edges together with a fork. Place empanadas slightly apart on an ungreased cookie sheet. Prick tops with fork. Bake at 400° for 20 minutes or until golden brown. If frozen, reheat empanadas uncovered at 400° for 7 to 8 minutes. Serve hot.

Sombreros

Can do ahead
Can be frozen

Yield: 20-24
Preparing: 20 min
Baking: 8-10 min

1	lb lean ground beef
2	Tb ice water
2	Tb taco seasoning

Filling

2	cups sour cream
1½	cups tortilla chips, crushed
5	Tb taco sauce
1	4-oz can ripe olives, chopped
8	oz sharp cheddar cheese, grated

Combine beef, water and taco seasoning. Press meat mixture onto bottom and sides of greased mini-muffin tins. Set aside. Combine sour cream, chips, taco sauce and olives. Spoon mixture into unbaked meat shells. Sprinkle with cheese. Bake 8-10 minutes in preheated 425° oven. Serve hot.

Baked Mexican Spread

Can partially do ahead

Serves: 10-12
Preparing: 30 min
Baking: 20-25 min

2 lbs ground beef	green onions, chopped
1 12-oz jar taco sauce	lettuce, chopped
2 16-oz cans refried beans	tomatoes, chopped
1 4-oz can chopped green chilies, drained	sour cream
	picante sauce (optional)
8 oz cheddar cheese, grated	tortilla chips

Brown ground beef. Drain well. Add taco sauce. Spread the refried beans in a 9″ × 13″ glass dish or a 2 quart casserole. Cover refried beans with ground beef mixture. Sprinkle with green chilies and cheese. Bake at 400° for 20-25 minutes. Remove from oven and top with green onions, lettuce and tomatoes. Garnish with sour cream. Top with picante sauce, if desired. Serve with tortilla chips.

Herbed Chicken Nuggets

Can do ahead
Can freeze

Yield: 100-120 pieces
Preparing: 30 min
Baking: 20 min

7-8 whole chicken breasts, boned	1½ tsp salt
2 cups dry bread crumbs, finely crushed	1 Tb plus 1 tsp dried thyme leaves
1 cup Parmesan cheese, grated	1 Tb plus 1 tsp dried basil
	1 cup margarine or butter, melted

Cut chicken into 1½ inch bite size pieces. Combine breadcrumbs, cheese, salt and herbs. Mix well. Dip chicken pieces in margarine and coat with breadcrumb mixture. Place on baking sheet in single layer. Bake at 400° for 20 minutes or until done. *Can be served with Honey Mustard Sauce. (See page 16)*

Honey Mustard Sauce

Can do ahead

Yield: 1¼ cups
Preparing: 5 min

⅓   cup vegetable oil
⅓   cup spicy brown or Dijon
     mustard
3-4 Tb honey

2   Tb dry sherry
1   Tb red wine vinegar
1   tsp lemon peel, grated

Mix all ingredients until well blended.

Spinach Wrapped Chicken with Oriental Dip

Can do ahead

Yield: 50-60 pieces
Preparing: 45 min
Cooking: 20 min

2   lbs chicken breasts,
    bone in
1   14-oz can chicken broth
¼   cup soy sauce
1   Tb Worcestershire sauce
1   lb fresh spinach

Oriental Dip
½   cup sour cream
1   tsp toasted sesame seed
¼   tsp ground ginger
2   tsp soy sauce
1   tsp Worcestershire sauce

Combine ingredients for Oriental Dip and refrigerate. Simmer the chicken breasts with broth, soy sauce and Worcestershire sauce just until fork tender. Remove chicken from broth and cool. Remove skin and bones and cut meat into 1 inch chunks. Wash spinach thoroughly, carefully remove stem ends and place whole leaves in a colander. Bring about 2 quarts of water to a boil and pour over leaves. Drain thoroughly and set aside to cool. To assemble, place a chunk of chicken at stem end of a large spinach leaf. Roll over once, fold leaf in on both sides and continue rolling around chicken. Secure end of leaf with wooden pick. Refrigerate until thoroughly chilled or overnight. Serve with Oriental Dip.

Chicken Mushroom Sandwiches

Can do ahead

Yield: 3-4 cups
Preparing: 30 min

2   cups cooked chicken, finely chopped
⅔   cup almonds, toasted, finely chopped
2   Tb instant minced onion
2   3-oz cans mushrooms, drained and chopped
1   cup celery, diced

½-1 tsp salt
¼   tsp pepper
1   tsp curry powder
1   cup mayonnaise
wheat bread rounds, light and dark

Combine all ingredients. Mix well. Spread on wheat bread rounds.

Chicken Almond Puffs

Can do ahead
Can freeze

Yield: 48
Preparing: 20 min
Cooking: 15 min

1   cup flour
1   cup chicken stock
2   tsp seasoned salt
⅛   tsp cayenne pepper
1   tsp celery seed
1   Tb dried parsley flakes

1   Tb Worcestershire sauce
½   cup butter or margarine
4   Eggs
½   cup cooked chicken, finely diced
2   Tb toasted almonds, chopped

Sift flour. In a saucepan over low heat, combine chicken stock, seasoned salt, cayenne pepper, celery seed, dried parsley flakes, Worcestershire sauce, and butter or margarine and bring to a boil. Add flour at once, stirring vigorously until mixture forms a ball and leaves the side of the pan (3 minutes). Remove from heat. Add eggs one at a time and beat thoroughly after each one. Continue beating until a thick dough is formed. Stir in chicken and almonds. Drop by small teaspoonfuls onto greased baking sheet. Bake at 450° for 10-15 minutes or until browned. Serve hot or freeze puffs in an air tight container. To thaw and crisp, put puffs on baking sheet and heat at 250° for 10-15 minutes.

Good served with Chinese mustard or apricot preserves.

Chinese Barbequed Riblets

Must do ahead

Yield: 4 lbs ribs
Preparing: 15 min
Baking: 1½ hr

4	lbs babyback ribs	1½	Tb sugar
1	cup soy sauce	⅛	tsp salt
½	cup water	1	clove garlic, minced
3	Tb red wine		

Have butcher trim excess fat from rack of ribs and split lengthwise. At home, score meat between individual ribs, being careful not to cut through. Combine all ingredients except ribs and stir well. Place ribs in a 9" × 13" pan. Pour mixture over ribs and marinate 1 hour or longer, stirring frequently. Place pan in 350° oven and bake ribs 1½ hours or until glazed. Turn frequently during baking time. Serve warm. Pour remaining marinade over ribs.

Pork Tenderloins

Must do ahead
Can freeze

Yield: 150 slices
Preparing: 15 min
Baking: 1 hr

1	cup soy sauce	2	Tb ground ginger
1	cup sesame seeds	1	Tb garlic powder
5	Tb sugar	2	pork tenderloins, 1 to
3	Tb onion, minced		1½ lbs each

Mix all ingredients except pork to make marinade. Marinate pork tenderloins at least 3 hours (better if longer). Turn once or twice during marinating time. Drain marinade and reserve. Bake tenderloins one hour at 375°. Cool and slice thinly. Put slices back in reserved marinade. May freeze at this point or heat for serving. Serve with party rye bread.

Party Ham

Can do ahead

**whole uncooked smoked ham
(20 lbs), do not trim fat**

Glaze
2   **cups brown sugar**
¼   **cup Coke or Pepsi**
½   **tsp ground cloves**

Bake unwrapped ham (fattest side up) on rack in roasting pan, uncovered, in 325° oven for 25 minutes per pound. Take ham out of oven one half hour before end of cooking time. Trim fat and rind, leaving about ¼ inch layer of fat.

Increase oven temperature to 400°. Combine ingredients for glaze; it will be a thick mixture. Spread glaze over ham. Put back in oven and cook for 15 minutes.

Cool for 1 hour before slicing. Serve with a variety of breads and condiments; artichoke or sweet Vidalia onion relish is quite good.

Ham Roll-Ups

Can do ahead

Yield: 5 dozen
Preparing: 30 min

1   **8-oz pkg cream cheese,
    softened**
½   **tsp Angostura bitters**

½   **Tb onion, finely chopped**
¾   **cup pecans, finely chopped**
¾   **lb ham, thinly sliced**

Combine first four ingredients. Spread on ham slices. Roll up. Refrigerate before slicing. Cut into circles.

Ham and Cheese Balls

Can do ahead

Yield: 50-60 balls
Preparing: 45 min

2 cups cooked ham, ground	4 eggs, beaten
2 cups bread crumbs	1 small onion, minced
1 cup Parmesan cheese, grated	4 Tb parsley flakes
	vegetable oil

Combine ham, 1 cup of the bread crumbs, Parmesan, eggs, onion and parsley. Shape mixture into bite size balls and roll in the remaining 1 cup of bread crumbs. Heat vegetable oil to 375° and fry until crisp. Serve on wooden picks with HOT MUSTARD SAUCE or HORSERADISH SAUCE.

Hot Mustard Sauce

Must do ahead

Yield: 1½ cups
Preparing: 20 min

½ cup dry mustard	2 eggs
⅓ cup sugar	2 Tb butter, softened
½ cup cider vinegar	

Combine mustard and sugar in top of double boiler. Add vinegar. Add eggs, one at a time, mixing well. Cook until thick. Remove from heat and beat in butter with a wire whisk. Serve chilled. Keeps indefinitely in refrigerator.

Horseradish Sauce

Can do ahead

Yield: 1 cup
Preparing: 5 min

1 cup sour cream	3-4 Tb horseradish
2 Tb mayonnaise	parsley, minced

Combine all ingredients.

Little Porkies

Can do ahead
Can freeze

Yield: 100
Preparing: 45 min
Baking: 1½ hrs

Meatballs
1 lb ground ham
1½ lbs ground pork (have
    meats ground together)
2 cups cracker crumbs
2 eggs
1 cup milk
½ cup lemon juice

Sauce
2 cups brown sugar
1 cup vinegar
1 cup water
1 tsp dry mustard

Combine all ingredients for meatballs. Roll mixture into bite size balls and place in a 9″ × 13″ pan. In a saucepan, combine sauce ingredients and heat until sugar and mustard are dissolved. Pour over meatballs. Bake at 325° for 1½ hours. Turn and baste balls at least once during cooking.

Italian Sausage Pick Ups

Serve immediately

1   8-oz can refrigerator cres-
     cent dinner rolls
2   Tb butter or margarine,
     melted
⅓   cup Parmesan cheese,
     grated

1-2 Tb oregano
8   Brown 'n Serve or
     precooked sausage links

Separate crescent dough into 4 rectangles, pressing perforations to seal. Brush each rectangle with butter. Combine Parmesan and oregano and sprinkle mixture over dough. Cut each rectangle to form 2 squares. Place a sausage link on each square and roll up. Cut each roll-up into 3-4 pieces. Secure with wooden picks. Place cut side down on ungreased cookie sheet. Bake at 375° for 12-15 minutes until brown.

Double Sausage and Pineapple Bits

Can do ahead
Can freeze pieces

2   lbs link sausage
1   lb hot bulk sausage

1   15-oz can pineapple
     chunks, including juice
1   cup + 2 Tb brown sugar

Slice sausages into ¼ inch pieces. Shape bulk sausage into balls 1 inch in diameter. In a skillet, brown both sausages. Drain fat, reserving 2 tablespoons (can be frozen at this point). Add pineapple with juice and brown sugar. Simmer, covered, for 30 minutes. Serve in chafing dish with cocktail picks.

Chutney Sausage Balls

Can do ahead

Yield: 24
Preparing: 30 min
Baking: 15 min

1	lb hot sausage	1	9 oz bottle Major Grey's Chutney, with mangos
1	cup sour cream	¼	cup sherry (optional)

Roll sausage into bite size balls. Bake at 350° for 15 minutes. Drain. Keep warm. In a double boiler, combine chutney and sour cream. Heat thoroughly. Pour over sausage balls. Serve from a chafing dish with wooden picks.

Rum Sausages

Can do ahead
Can freeze

Yield: 30 pieces
Preparing: 30 min

3	pkgs Brown N'Serve sausage or any precooked sausage links	⅓	cup dark rum
1	cup dark brown sugar	1	Tb soy sauce
			dash Worcestershire sauce

Cut each sausage into 3 pieces. Place in large skillet and brown. Remove sausages and drain all fat. Allow pan to cool slightly. Add brown sugar, rum, soy sauce and Worcestershire sauce. Heat until blended. Return sausages to pan and simmer until well glazed. Serve from a chafing dish with wooden picks.

Pepperoni Dip

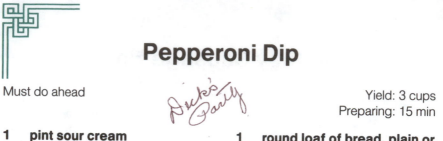

1   pint sour cream
½   lb pepperoni, finely
     chopped

1   round loaf of bread, plain or
     rye

Combine sour cream and pepperoni. Store covered in refrigerator for 2 days. To serve, allow dip to come to room temperature. Carefully hollow out round loaf of bread, leaving 1 inch around sides and across bottom of loaf. Tear this center section of bread into bite size pieces. Place in hollowed out loaf and surround with bread pieces.

Kielbasa En Croute

Serve immediately

Serves: 8
Preparing: 30 min
Baking: 15-20 min

1   8-oz can crescent rolls
1   10-inch Kielbasa or pepper-
     oni (approximately ⅓ lb)

1   egg yolk, beaten
flour

Preheat oven to 350°. On an ungreased cookie sheet, roll crescent dough in one piece and pinch perforations closed. Brush Kielbasa or pepperoni with egg yolk. Roll in flour. Place on dough and roll up, covering completely. Tuck ends in neatly. Bake 15-20 minutes or until golden brown. Slice and serve immediately with Dijon or other mustard or barbecue sauce.

Bacon Crescents

Can partially do ahead

1	8-oz can crescent dinner rolls	½	lb bacon, cooked and crumbled
½	cup sour cream		Parmesan cheese (optional)
½	tsp onion salt		chives (optional)

Separate dinner rolls into eight triangles. Combine sour cream and onion salt. Spread mixture on dough triangles. Sprinkle with bacon and Parmesan cheese and chives if desired. Cut each triangle into three wedges. Roll each wedge to form a small crescent. Place on a cookie sheet. Bake at 375° for 15 minutes. Serve hot.

Hidden Treasures

Must do ahead

Serves: 25
Preparing: 1 hr 15 min

2   cups mayonnaise
½   cup horseradish sauce
2   tsp spicy mustard
2   tsp lemon juice, fresh
½   tsp salt
1   pint small cherry tomatoes
1   lb medium shrimp, cleaned
     and cooked
1   lb bay scallops, cooked

1   6-oz can black olives,
     pitted
1   6-oz can whole mushrooms
1   8-oz can water chestnuts
½   head cauliflower, cut into
     florets
1   small green pepper, cut
     into bite size pieces

One day before serving, combine mayonnaise with horseradish sauce, mustard, lemon juice and salt. Add remaining ingredients except cauliflower and green pepper. Refrigerate. Drain sauce, before serving, and add cauliflower and green pepper. Serve with wooden picks or bamboo skewers. *Avocado or cucumber cubes are tasty variations. Can serve as seafood salad on bed of lettuce.*

Seafood Mousse

Must do ahead

1½ envelopes gelatin
¼ cup dry vermouth
1 can cream of mushroom soup, undiluted
1 8-oz pkg cream cheese, softened
1 cup mayonnaise
1 cup celery, finely chopped
1 medium onion, minced
1 tsp Worcestershire sauce
1 tsp horseradish
1 lb crabmeat (shrimp, lobster or salmon)

Soften gelatin in vermouth. Heat soup (do not boil) and add softened gelatin, dissolving thoroughly. Set aside. With a mixer, combine cream cheese with mayonnaise. Add celery and onion. Add gelatin mixture, Worcestershire sauce and horseradish. Combine well. Stir in crabmeat. Pour into greased 5 cup mold. Garnish and serve with melba toast or a bland cracker.

Marinated Oysters

Must do ahead

½ gallon oysters, drained
3-4 cloves garlic, minced
2 medium onions, finely chopped
salt, pepper, hot sauce to taste
juice of 2 large lemons
¼ cup dry white wine
1 cup Italian salad dressing

Place oysters in a large container. Add remaining ingredients. Stir. Cover and marinate in refrigerator overnight. Stir at least twice. Drain before serving. Serve with crackers.

Nutty Oysters

Serve immediately
Can partially do ahead

Yield: 40 balls
Preparing: 1 hr
Cooking: Deep fry
2-3 min

2   12-oz cans oysters
¼   cup almonds, blanched,
     toasted, chopped
4   cups fine, soft bread
     crumbs
1   egg, beaten
1   Tb onion, chopped

1   Tb parsley, chopped
¼   tsp salt
dash of nutmeg
dash of pepper
vegetable oil
1   cup cocktail sauce

Drain oysters thoroughly and chop. Combine almonds, 3 cups of the bread crumbs, egg, onion, parsley, seasonings and oysters. Mix well. Shape mixture into small balls and roll to coat in remaining bread crumbs. Heat vegetable oil to 375°. Deep fry for 2-3 minutes until golden brown. Drain on absorbent paper. Heat cocktail sauce and serve with the oyster balls. Serve hot.

Smoked Oyster Spread

Must do ahead

Yield: 2 cups
Preparing: 15 min

1   8-oz pkg cream cheese,
     softened
½   cup mayonnaise
¼-½ cup ripe olives, chopped
1   tsp Worcestershire sauce

2   tsp lemon juice
1   tsp hot sauce
1   can smoked oysters,
     drained and chopped
unsalted crackers
cucumber slices

Combine cream cheese and mayonnaise. Add remaining ingredients except crackers and cucumbers. Chill. Serve on unsalted crackers or cucumber slices.

Shrimp Taiwan

Must do ahead

Yield: 24
Preparing: 30 min
Baking: 20 min

12	water chestnuts	½	cup soy sauce
12	slices bacon, thinly sliced	½	cup honey
24	raw shrimp, cleaned and deveined	2	Tb sherry
		2	garlic cloves, minced

Two days before serving, halve water chestnuts and bacon slices. Place water chestnuts inside curve of each shrimp. Wrap with bacon and secure with wooden picks. Combine soy sauce, honey, sherry and garlic. Pour over shrimp and refrigerate for 2 days. Preheat oven to 400°. Bake shrimp on baking sheet for 10 minutes. Turn shrimp. Continue baking for 10 additional minutes or until crisp and brown. Serve with cocktail picks.

Barbecued Shrimp

Must partially do ahead

Yield: ½ lb
Preparing: 10-15 min
Cooking: 10-15 min

3	Tb lemon juice	3	Tb minced onion
1	Tb Worcestershire sauce	1½	Tb olive oil
1	tsp prepared hot mustard	1	Tb brown sugar
⅛	tsp salt	½	lb shrimp, peeled and deveined
½	cup catsup		
¼	cup water		

Combine all ingredients except shrimp. Bring to a boil, reduce heat and simmer 10 minutes. Pour over shrimp and refrigerate at least 4 hours. Thread shrimp on metal skewers. Grill over hot coals for 10-15 minutes. Turn and baste frequently. Do not overcook!

Spiced Shrimp

Must do ahead

Yield: 2 qts
Preparing: 45 min
Cooking: 10 min

1	lb fresh mushrooms, quartered	½	tsp peppercorns
1	cup water	⅛	tsp nutmeg
⅓	cup olive oil	7-8	scallions, chopped, including tops
⅔	cup vinegar	2	bay leaves
2	Tb fresh lemon juice	¾	cup small pimento stuffed olives
2	cloves garlic, halved		
1¼	tsp salt	2	lbs medium shrimp, cooked and cleaned
½	tsp thyme		

In a saucepan, combine all ingredients except shrimp and olives. Bring to a boil. Reduce heat and simmer covered for 5 minutes. Pour into a bowl. Add olives and shrimp. Cool. Cover and chill 6-8 hours or overnight. Strain well before serving. Serve with party picks.

Shrimp-Artichoke Marinade

Must do ahead

Yield: 24
Preparing: 30 min

½	cup olive oil	2	Tb parsley, chopped
¼	cup peanut oil	2	Tb shallots, chopped
¼	cup wine vinegar	24	large shrimp, cooked and cleaned
1	egg yolk, beaten		
2	Tb Dijon mustard	1	14-oz can artichoke hearts, halved if large
2	Tb chives, chopped		red tipped lettuce

One day before serving, combine olive oil, peanut oil and vinegar. Add beaten egg yolk and mustard. Mix well. Add remaining ingredients except lettuce. Chill 8 hours or overnight, stirring occasionally. Drain well before serving. Line serving dish with red tipped lettuce. Fill with shrimp-artichoke mixture. Serve with cocktail picks.

Shrimp in Fresh Dill Marinade

Must do ahead

Yield: 40-50
Preparing: 1 hr
Cooking: 3-4 min

1 tsp dill seed
1 lemon, sliced
2½ lbs shrimp in shell

Marinade
½ cup olive oil
½ cup white wine
2 Tb fresh dill, chopped or
3 tsp dried
1 tsp pepper, fresh ground
dash garlic powder
2 drops hot sauce
½ cup lemon juice
1 Tb chives
salt to taste

Combine dill seed and lemon slices in salted water and bring to a boil. Add shrimp. Simmer 3-4 minutes until pink. Drain and chill shrimp. Peel and devein. Place in bowl. Combine marinade and pour marinade over shrimp. Cover. Refrigerate for 24 hours.

Shrimp Butter

Can do ahead

Yield: 2 ½ cups
Preparing: 20 min

½ cup butter, softened
1 8-oz pkg cream cheese, softened
4 Tb mayonnaise
8-12 oz shrimp, cleaned, cooked and minced

½-1 tsp garlic salt
salt and pepper to taste
2-3 Tb onion, finely minced
dash lemon juice

Combine butter, cream cheese and mayonnaise. Blend shrimp with butter mixture. Add seasonings to taste. Serve with crackers or as a canape spread on toast rounds.

Crab Mornay

Can do ahead

Yield: 1 qt
Preparing: 30 min

½   cup butter or margarine
1   small bunch green onions,
    chopped
½   cup parsley, finely
    chopped
2   Tb flour

1   pint half and half
½   lb Swiss cheese
1   Tb sherry
salt to taste
red pepper to taste
1   lb crabmeat

In a heavy bottomed 2 quart saucepan over low heat, melt butter. Sauté onions and parsley just until soft. Blend in flour, half and half, and cheese. When cheese has melted, add sherry, salt and red pepper. Fold in crabmeat. Serve in chafing dish with crackers.

Buried Crab

Can do ahead

Serves: 20
Preparing: 20 min

1   lb fresh crabmeat
2   8-oz pkgs cream cheese,
    softened
2   Tb Worcestershire sauce
1   small onion, grated
pinch garlic salt

1   Tb lemon juice
2   Tb mayonnaise
6   oz seafood cocktail or chili
    sauce
parsley

Carefully pick through crabmeat. Set aside. Combine cream cheese, Worcestershire, onion, garlic salt, lemon juice and mayonnaise. Spread on platter. Spoon the seafood sauce over this mixture. Layer the crabmeat over the sauce. Sprinkle parsley on top. Serve with butter crackers or water biscuits.

Crabmeat Pâté

Must do ahead

Yield: 2-3 cups
Preparing: 15 min

½ cup butter
2 Tb lemon juice
½ cup mayonnaise
⅓ cup Parmesan cheese,
   freshly grated
3 hard boiled eggs
1½ tsp horseradish

½ tsp salt
¼ tsp garlic powder
dash white pepper
¼ cup onion, minced
¼ cup parsley, chopped
8 oz crabmeat, fresh if
   possible

Whip butter, lemon juice and mayonnaise until fluffy. Add cheese, egg yolks and seasonings. Chop egg whites and add onion, crab and parsley. Combine two mixtures. Chill several hours or overnight. Serve from an earthenware crock or mounded on a platter surrounded with crackers.

Hot Crab Spread

Can do ahead

Yield: 2 qts
Preparing: 10 min
Baking: 20-30 min

3 8-oz pkgs cream cheese,
   softened
2 lbs crabmeat, fresh or
   frozen

¾ cup onion, minced
½ cup cheddar cheese,
   grated

Combine cream cheese, crabmeat and onion. Place in 2 quart casserole, top with cheddar cheese. Bake at 350° for 20-30 minutes. Serve with rye wafers or Melba rounds.

Crab Verde

Can do ahead
Can freeze

Yield: 3 cups
Preparing: 10 min

1	10-oz pkg frozen, chopped spinach
8	oz crabmeat grated
1	small bunch green onions, chopped

1-2	cloves garlic, minced
⅓	cup Parmesan cheese, grated
½	cup mayonnaise

Microwave spinach on high for 4 minutes until warm. Drain. Thoroughly squeeze out moisture. Combine with remaining ingredients. Heat at 80% power for 2 minutes. Serve in a chafing dish with Triscuits or melba rounds.

Velvet Crab

Can partially do ahead

Yield: 4-5 cups
Preparing: 20 min

1	lb fresh crabmeat, well picked
1	8-oz pkg cream cheese
1	8-oz carton sour cream
4	Tb mayonnaise
½	tsp lemon juice

1	Tb Worcestershire sauce
1	tsp dry mustard
3	shakes garlic salt
½	cup sharp cheese, grated
2	Tb cream sherry
	milk to make creamy

Pick the crabmeat carefully. Place cream cheese and sour cream in microwave on defrost for 4 minutes. Whip with whisk. Add all ingredients except crabmeat. Mix well. Add crabmeat by folding in gently. Heat in a double boiler. Serve in a chafing dish. Serve with bland crackers.

Crabmeat Ring

Must do ahead

Yield: 3 cups
Preparing: 15 min

1   **lb crabmeat, fresh or frozen**
1   **8-oz pkg cream cheese,
softened**
dash of hot sauce

grind of black pepper
1   **tsp chives**
dash Worcestershire sauce

Combine all ingredients and put into 3 cup ring mold. Chill 6 to 8 hours. Unmold and serve, filling center with Seafood Cocktail Sauce. Spread on crackers.

Seafood Cocktail Sauce

Can do ahead

Yield: ½ cup
Preparing: 15 min

6   **Tb catsup**
2   **Tb lemon juice**
1½ **Tb horseradish**
¼   **tsp onion, grated**

1   **tsp Worcestershire sauce**
2   **drops hot sauce**
salt to taste

Combine all ingredients and chill. Serve with cocktail seafood dishes.

Crab or Shrimp Wedges

Must do ahead
Must freeze

Yield: 72 triangles
Preparing: 20 min
Cooking: 5 min

½   cup butter, softened
1   7-oz jar Old English Cheese
    Spread
1½ tsp mayonnaise
½   tsp garlic salt
½   tsp seasoned salt

1   Tb onion, grated
1   Tb parsley flakes
1   7-oz can crabmeat or
    shrimp, drained
6   English muffins, split

Combine all ingredients except seafood and muffins. Gently stir in crabmeat or shrimp. Spread mixture on split muffins and place on cookie sheet to freeze. When frozen, cut each muffin into 6 wedges. Bag and freeze until needed. When ready to serve, take out amount needed and place on a cookie sheet. Broil until slightly bubbly and browned. Serve immediately.

Crab Roll-Ups

Must do ahead
Can freeze

Yield: 75
Preparing: 45 min
Cooking: 5 min

8   oz pasteurized cheese
2   cups butter
2   6-oz cans crabmeat

25 slices white bread
    sesame seeds

Melt cheese with 1 cup of the butter in top of double broiler or in microwave, stirring to mix well. Cool. Add crabmeat, stirring until mixture is spreadable. Cut crusts off bread and flatten with rolling pin. Spread mixture on bread and roll up. Melt remaining 1 cup butter. Dip rolls in the butter and sprinkle with sesame seeds. Place rolls in shallow baking pan. Freeze. To serve, thaw slightly and cut each roll into thirds. Broil 6 to 8 inches from heat until brown.

Crab-Swiss Rounds

Serve immediately

Yield: 36 rounds
Preparing: 20 min
Baking: 10-12 min

1   **7-oz can crabmeat, drained**
4   **oz Swiss cheese, grated**
½   **cup mayonnaise**
2   **Tb green onion, finely chopped**
1   **tsp lemon juice**

¼   **tsp curry powder**
1   **12-roll pkg refrigerated flaky rolls**
1   **8-oz can water chestnuts, sliced and drained**

Mix first 6 ingredients well. Separate each roll into 3 layers. Place on greased cookie sheet. Spread crab mixture on rolls. Top with water chestnuts. Bake in 400° oven for 10-12 minutes.

Salmon Pâté

Must do ahead

Yield: 2 cups
Preparing: 10 min

1   **16-oz can salmon, deboned**
1   **clove garlic, quartered**

juice of 1 lemon
½   **cup butter, melted**

Puree salmon in food processor, using steel blade. Add garlic and lemon juice. Pour in butter. This procedure will take approximately one minute. Put pâté in serving crock. Cover and refrigerate at least 6 hours. Serve with Bremner crackers.

Salmon Mold

Must do ahead

Yield: 6 cup mold
Preparing: 45 min

1   16-oz can pink salmon,
    drained, deboned, flaked
    (reserve liquid)
2   envelopes unflavored
    gelatin
2   cups mayonnaise
½   cup chili sauce
2   Tb lemon juice
2   Tb Worcestershire sauce

½   tsp dried dill weed
¼   tsp black pepper
1   6½-oz can white tuna in
    water, drained and flaked
4   hard boiled eggs, chopped
½   cup pimento stuffed
    olives, chopped
¼   cup onion, finely chopped

Drain salmon, reserving liquid. Add water, if necessary, to equal ½ cup of liquid. Combine gelatin and salmon liquid in heat-proof measuring cup. Place cup in a saucepan of hot water and stir to dissolve gelatin. Transfer gelatin mixture to a large 3 quart mixing bowl. Gently stir in mayonnaise, chili sauce, lemon juice, Worcestershire sauce, dill weed and pepper. Fold in salmon, tuna, eggs, olives and onion. Turn into a greased 6 cup mold (fish mold preferred). Chill until firm. Unmold on a platter. Garnish with additional sliced olives, pimento strips, hard boiled eggs and parsley. Serve with thin crackers.

Hot Clam and Cheese Dip

Can do ahead

Yield: 1½ cups
Preparing: 20 min

1   medium onion, finely
    chopped
½   green pepper, finely
    chopped
3   Tb butter
2   6½-oz cans minced clams,
    drained

2   Tb catsup
1   tsp Worcestershire sauce
1   Tb sherry
½   lb pasteurized cheese,
    diced

Sauté onion and green pepper in butter until vegetables are soft. Add remaining ingredients and heat, stirring until cheese melts. Serve from chafing dish with melba rounds, dill pickle slices or chips.

Pecan Clam Roll

Must do ahead

Serves: 15
Preparing: 20 min

2   6½-oz cans clams, drained
    and minced
1   Tb lemon juice
1   tsp prepared mustard
1   tsp Worcestershire sauce
2   Tb fresh parsley, chopped

2   Tb onion, finely chopped
1   2-oz jar pimentos, drained
⅓   cup saltines, crushed
2   8-oz pkgs cream cheese,
    softened
½   cup pecans, chopped

Combine all ingredients except pecans. Form into a ball or log. Roll in pecans. Refrigerate several hours. Bring to room temperature. Serve with crackers.

Mini-Quiche Rockefeller

Must partially do ahead

Yield: 48
Preparing: 1 hr.
Baking: 28-32 min

Pastry
1   cup butter, softened
6   oz cream cheese, softened
2½ cups flour, unsifted
¼   tsp salt

Filling
1	lb bulk sausage	¼ tsp oregano
½	cup onion, chopped	½ cup mushrooms, chopped
3	eggs, beaten	1½ cups Monterey Jack
¼	cup milk	cheese, grated
6	oz spinach, chopped	Parmesan cheese

Pastry: Cream together butter and cheese until well combined. Add flour and salt. Shape into 2 rolls approximately 2 inches in diameter. Wrap and chill overnight. Next day slice pastry approximately 1 inch thick and press into small muffin tins, being careful not to make dough too thick. It will rise slightly. Do not make rims. Bake 8 minutes in 400° preheated oven.

Filling: Preheat oven to 350°. Brown sausage and onions. Drain. Add remaining ingredients except Parmesan. Pour mixture into pastries and sprinkle with Parmesan cheese. Bake 20-25 minutes in 350° oven.

Cheese Squares Florentine

Can freeze

Yield: 4-5 dozen
Preparing: 20 min
Baking: 30 min

1	10-oz pkg frozen, chopped spinach, thawed and drained	2	eggs, slightly beaten
1	cup flour	1	cup milk
1	tsp salt	3	Tb butter, melted
1	tsp baking powder	1	lb sharp cheddar cheese, grated
		½	cup onion, finely minced

Squeeze spinach dry. Set aside. Combine flour, salt and baking powder in large bowl. Add eggs, milk, butter, cheese and onion. Add spinach and blend well. Spread evenly in greased 9″ × 13″ baking dish. Bake at 325° for 30-35 minutes. Cool slightly before cutting into small squares.

Bake frozen squares at 350° for 15-20 minutes or until heated thoroughly.

Cheese Olive Hors d'Oeuvres

Can freeze

Yield: 4 doz
Preparing: 15 min
Baking: 35 min

1	6-oz jar salad olives, drained and chopped	1	tsp Tabasco
5	eggs, beaten	1	tsp Worcestershire sauce
1	lb medium cheddar cheese, grated	½	tsp garlic powder to taste (optional)

Spray a 9″x13″ pan with a non-stick coating. Cover the bottom with olives. Combine eggs, cheese and seasonings. Pour over olives. Bake at 350° for 35 minutes (can be frozen in pan at this point). Cut into 1 inch squares and serve warm.

Cream Cheese Pinwheels

Can partially do ahead

Yield: 48 pieces
Preparing: 15 min
Baking: 10-15 min

1   **8-oz pkg crescent rolls**
1   **8-oz pkg cream cheese, softened**

1   **1-oz pkg buttermilk salad dressing mix**

Unroll crescent rolls, spread flat into two rectangles and press the seams together. Beat cream cheese until smooth. Add the salad dressing and mix well. Spread mixture on rectangles. Roll up jelly roll style. Wrap tightly in waxed paper. Chill until firm. Slice thinly. Bake at 350° for 10-15 minutes or until brown. Serve warm.

Cheese Wellington

Serve immediately

Serves: 8
Preparing: 10 min
Baking: 20-30 min

1   **8-count can crescent dinner rolls**

1   **12-oz pkg Monterey Jack cheese**

Remove rolls from package and squeeze perforations together making one solid rectangle. Make sure there are no holes. Place block of cheese in the middle of the rectangle. Wrap like a package. Place on an oven-proof dish that will be suitable for serving. Bake at 350° for 20-30 minutes or until golden brown (looks like a loaf). Serve with crackers and fruit.

Blue Cheesy Bread Bites

Serve immediately

Yield: 40
Preparing: 20 min
Baking: 10 min

1   10-count can refrigerated
    biscuits

1   4-oz pkg blue cheese
½   cup butter

Cut each biscuit into fourths to make 40. Melt butter and cheese together. Pour over biscuit pieces, coating each piece. Bake 10 minutes or according to directions on biscuit can.

Golden Gouda in Puff Pastry

Can freeze

Serves: 10-12
Preparing: 20 min
Baking: 30 min

1   17¼-oz pkg puff pastry
2   8-oz rounds gouda cheese

Dijon or champagne mustard

Thaw pastry. Peel gouda and spread with mustard. Wrap each cheese with a sheet of pastry. Place on greased cookie sheet. Bake at 400° for 30 minutes or until golden brown. Cut into wedges and serve with fruit.

Apricot Brie Wrapped in Phyllo

Can partially do ahead

Serves: 20-25
Preparing: 25 min
Baking: 20-25 min

1-½ cups sweet butter, melted
11-12 sheets phyllo pastry

1   whole Brie, approximately
    5 lbs
1   12-oz jar apricot preserves

Butter jelly roll pan, making sure it is large enough for round of Brie. Lay 5 sheets of phyllo on buttered pan, staggering layers to create a circle and brushing butter between each layer. Place Brie on top of phyllo and spread top and sides with apricot preserves. Fold phyllo over and up around the cheese. Cover top of cheese with 6 sheets of phyllo, brushing butter on each. Tuck ends of pastry under cheese. Brush top & sides with butter. Fold last sheet of phyllo in 1 inch wide strip. Brush with butter and form flower shape. Center flower on top and again brush with butter. Bake at 350° for 20-25 minutes. Let stand 30 minutes before serving.

Raffetto's Spread

Must do ahead

Yield: 2 cups
Preparing: 10 min

2   8-oz pkgs cream cheese
½   tsp curry
½   tsp dry mustard

6-oz jar Raffetto Chut-nut
    Chutney
2   2-oz bags sliced almonds

Combine cream cheese, curry, dry mustard and chutney. Shape into a ball. Chill. Roll in slivered almonds before serving. Serve with apple slices or crackers.

Curried Chutney Spread

Can partially do ahead

Yield: 2 cups
Preparing: 10 min

1 **8-oz pkg cream cheese, softened**
4 **oz sharp cheddar cheese, grated**
½ **tsp curry powder**

¼ **tsp salt**
3 **Tb sherry**
½ **cup chutney, chopped**
2 **large green onions, finely chopped**

Combine first five ingredients. Spread in a shallow serving dish. Top with chutney and green onions. Serve with Bremner Wafers. *Can substitute white wine for sherry.*

Turkey Cheese Ball

Must do ahead

Yield: 2½ cups
Preparing: 15 min

1 **8-oz pkg cream cheese, softened**
1 **cup cooked turkey or chicken, finely chopped**
¾ **cup almonds, toasted and finely chopped**

⅓ **cup mayonnaise**
2 **Tb chutney, chopped**
1 **Tb curry**
¼ **tsp salt**
chopped parsley

Combine all ingredients except parsley. Chill several hours. Shape into ball. Roll in parsley. Serve with crackers. Garnish by surrounding with freshly cooked artichoke petals.

Daffodil Dip

Can do ahead

Yield: 2 cups
Preparing: 15-20 min

½   cup mayonnaise
8   oz cream cheese, softened
2   eggs, hard-boiled and
     finely chopped
2   Tb onion, chopped

¼   tsp salt
pepper to taste
⅛   tsp garlic powder
parsley to taste

Combine mayonnaise and cream cheese. Add eggs, onion, salt, pepper, garlic powder and parsley. Mix well. Serve with bread sticks, crackers or fresh vegetables.

Frosted Egg Salad

Must do ahead

Yield: 3½ cup mold
Preparing: 45 min

8   hard boiled eggs, finely
     chopped
½   cup butter, softened
1   Tb green onion, minced
⅛   tsp pepper
¾   tsp salt

½   tsp lemon juice
⅛   tsp curry powder (optional)
⅓   cup sour cream
choice of chopped chives or
small jar black caviar, drained
parsley for garnish

Combine eggs, butter, onion, salt, pepper, lemon juice and curry powder in a food processor. Puree. Line a 3½ cup mold with plastic wrap, leaving extra wrap for handles. Pack mixture into mold. Cover and refrigerate for 3 hours or until set. Take out 2 hours before unmolding. Unmold onto plate. Spread with sour cream, sprinkle with chives or caviar and garnish with parsley. Serve with crackers or trimmed thin bread.

Bull's Eye

Must do ahead

Base
1	cup cottage cheese
1	cup sour cream
1	tsp lemon juice
1	tsp Worcestershire sauce
¼	tsp seasoned salt
1	envelope unflavored gelatin
¼	cup dry white wine

Garnish
3	hard boiled eggs
3	green onions, finely chopped
1	2-oz jar red caviar, drained
1	4-oz jar black caviar, drained
3	lemon slices

Base: Combine the first 5 ingredients in blender or food processor and blend until smooth. Sprinkle gelatin over wine and heat in microwave or on the stove just until dissolved. Add to cottage cheese mixture. Pour into nine or ten inch quiche or spring form pan. Refrigerate for 4 to 6 hours until firm.

Garnish: Separate egg yolks from whites. Chop yolks, whites and onions separately. Set aside. To serve, invert base mixture onto serving platter, remove pan. Spread red caviar in small solid circle on center of mold, forming the "bull's eye" of the "target". Sprinkle egg yolks in a circle around caviar. Continue forming concentric circles with black caviar, egg whites and then onions. Chill. Garnish with lemon slices. Serve with crackers.

Cheese-Caviar Spread

Must do ahead

Serves: 8-10
Preparing: 20 min

2 8-oz containers cream
   cheese with chives,
   softened
3 Tb chives, chopped
   (fresh if available)
mayonnaise
1 2-oz jar caviar, well drained
   and rinsed

1 Tb onion, minced
1 Tb lemon juice
3-4 hard cooked egg yolks,
   chopped
parsley or lemon sliced

Combine cream cheese with chives and chives until smooth. Spread in shallow serving dish and chill until firm. Spread with a thin layer of mayonnaise. When ready to serve, cover entire surface with caviar mixed with onion and lemon juice. Sprinkle with egg yolks. Garnish with parsley or lemon slices. Serve with crackers.

Olive and Blue Cheese Ball

Must do ahead

Yield: 2 cups
Preparing: 15 min

1 8-oz pkg cream cheese,
   softened
1 4-oz pkg blue cheese,
   crumbled
2 Tb butter, softened

½ cup pimento stuffed olives,
   chopped
1 tsp chives
chopped walnuts (optional)

Combine cream cheese, blue cheese and butter. Blend thoroughly. Add olives and chives. Chill. Form into a ball. Roll in walnuts if desired. Serve with bland crackers.

Ginger Cheese Ball

Must do ahead

Yield: 3-4 cups
Preparing: 30 min

3   8-oz pkgs cream cheese, softened
1   cup crystallized preserved ginger, finely chopped

1   5-oz can chopped, roasted almonds
Swedish gingersnaps

Combine cream cheese and ginger. Chill. Shape into ball. Refrigerate, covered, 6 hours or overnight. Roll ball in chopped almonds until completely covered. Serve with Swedish ginger snaps.

Pepper Jelly Mold

Must do ahead

Yield: 3½ cups
Preparing: 30 min

2   8-oz pkgs cream cheese, softened
1   cup hot pepper jelly

1   Tb unflavored gelatin
¼   cup cold milk
½   cup boiling milk

With a mixer, beat cream cheese until smooth. Add jelly. Blend well. Soften gelatin in cold milk, add boiling milk. Stir until dissolved. Combine with cream cheese mixture. Pour into 3½ cup mold. Chill. Unmold and serve with crackers. Can be done up to 2 days before serving.

Can be seasonally appropriate by using red or green jelly. Color of mold can be deepened with food coloring if desired. Garnish with fresh parsley or native greenery.

Spicy Pimento Cheese

Can do ahead

Yield: 6 cups
Preparing:15-20 min

1   medium onion, grated
20 oz extra sharp cheese, grated
2   cups mayonnaise
1   Tb Worcestershire sauce
½ tsp salt or more to taste

1   Tb red pepper or more
1   6-oz jar pimentos, sliced
1   Tb juice from pimento jar
hot pepper jelly
chopped pecans, optional

Toss cheese and onion together in large bowl. Add remaining ingredients and mix by hand. Top with hot pepper jelly and serve with crackers.

Can add chopped pecans.

Blue Cheese Dip

Can do ahead

Yield: 3 cups
Preparing: 10 min

1   clove garlic, minced
2   Tb mayonnaise
½ tsp salt
juice of one small lemon
1   16-oz carton sour cream

¾-1 cup blue cheese, crumbled
black pepper
paprika

Combine garlic, mayonnaise and salt. Squeeze lemon juice into mixture and stir. Fold mixture into sour cream. Gently add crumbled blue cheese. Add pepper and paprika to taste. Serve with vegetables or chip. *Can be used as a salad dressing, a garnish for baked potatoes or a dip for beef fondue.*

Extra Easy Taco Dip

Can do ahead

Yield: 1 1/2 cups
Preparing: 15 min

1	**8-oz pkg cream cheese, softened**
4	**oz taco sauce**
	lemon juice to taste

garlic salt to taste
hot sauce to taste
corn chips

Blend softened cream cheese and taco sauce in food processor or mixer. Season to taste. Serve with corn chips.

South of the Border Dip

Can do ahead

Yield: 5 cups
Preparing: 20 min
Baking: 20-25 min

1	**8-oz pkg cream cheese, softened**
1	**8-oz carton sour cream**
1	**10½-oz can jalapeño bean dip**
1	**1¼-oz pkg chili seasoning mix**
¼	**cup taco sauce**

1	**green onion, finely chopped**
1	**cup Monterey Jack cheese, grated**
1½	**cups cheddar cheese, grated**
⅓	**cup black olives, sliced**
	corn chips

Beat softened cream cheese and sour cream together. Stir in bean dip, chili mix, taco sauce, onion, Monterey Jack cheese and 1 cup cheddar cheese. Pour mixture into baking dish and bake at 325° for 20 minutes until the cheese has melted. Remove from oven and top with black olives and the remaining ½ cup cheddar cheese. Return to oven until cheese has melted. Serve with corn chips.

Green Chili Bites

Can freeze

Yield: 4-5 dozen
Preparing: 10 min
Baking: 30 min

1   4-oz can mild green chilies,
    drained and chopped
1½ lb sharp cheddar cheese,
    grated

9   eggs
    hot sauce to taste (optional)

Place chilies in bottom of a buttered 9″ × 13″ pan. Sprinkle with cheese. Beat eggs until fluffy and pour over cheese. Bake uncovered at 350° for 30 minutes or until firm. Cut into 1 inch squares and serve hot. Can be frozen and thawed in refrigerator. Warm 10 minutes at 200°. *Can substitute 10 oz can Rotel tomatoes and green chilies, drained, for chilies.*

Chili Con Queso

Can do ahead

Yield: 1 qt
Preparing: 15 min

1   lb pasteurized cheese,
    melted
1   cup mayonnaise
1   10-oz can tomatoes and
    green chilies, drained and
    chopped

⅓   cup onion, grated
2-3 drops hot sauce
    tortilla chips

Melt cheese in double boiler or microwave (instructions below). Remove from heat. Add remaining ingredients. Mix well. Serve in chafing dish with tortilla chips.

Microwave: Cut cheese into cubes. Place cheese and tomatoes in 2 qt casserole for 10-12 minutes on medium power until cheese is melted. Add remaining ingredients. *Leftover dip is delicious served as a sauce over cooked vegetables such as broccoli and cauliflower.*

Mexican Cheesecake

Must do ahead

Serves: 12-14
Preparing: 20 min
Baking: 8-10 min

2	cups corn chips, crushed
¼	cup butter, melted
2	16-oz cans refried beans
1	pkg taco seasoning
3	medium avocados, mashed
2	Tb lemon juice
½	tsp salt
½	tsp pepper
1	cup sour cream
½	cup mayonnaise

taco sauce to taste (optional)
1   cup green onions, chopped
3   medium tomatoes,
      chopped and drained
1   6-oz can ripe olives, sliced
6   oz cheddar cheese, grated
6   oz Monterey Jack cheese,
      grated
tortilla chips

Mix corn chips with melted butter. Press on bottom and sides of 9″ spring form pan. Bake at 350° for 8-10 minutes; cool. Mix together refried beans and one half of taco seasoning. Spread lightly on the corn chip crust. Mash avocados with lemon juice, salt and pepper. Spread over beans. Mix sour cream, mayonnaise, and remaining taco seasoning. If spicier flavoring is desired, add taco sauce. Spread sour cream mixture over avocado mixture. Sprinkle onions, tomatoes, olives and cheeses over sour cream. Chill several hours before serving. To serve, remove side of pan. Center cheesecake on platter and surround with tortilla chips. *Can omit the corn chip crust and layer on a large serving plate.*

Artichoke Hearts with Caviar

Can do ahead

Serves: 10
Preparing: 15 min

1   2-oz jar caviar
1   8-oz pkg cream cheese,
    softened
2   Tb sour cream
2   tsp mayonnaise
1   tsp lemon juice

1   8½-oz can artichoke
    hearts, drained and
    chopped
2   tsp onion, grated
1   small clove garlic, minced

In a fine sieve, gently rinse caviar under cold water. Drain. Set aside. Combine cream cheese, sour cream, mayonnaise and lemon juice. Add artichoke hearts, onion and garlic. Shape into a mound and spread with caviar. Serve with crackers.

Blue Cheese Dish Artichokes

Serve immediately

Serves: 6-8
Preparing: 20 min

¾   cup butter
4   oz blue cheese, crumbled
2   Tb lemon juice

2   16-oz cans artichoke
     hearts, drained and
     quartered

Melt butter and blue cheese over low heat. Add lemon juice and stir well. Add artichoke hearts and heat thoroughly. Transfer to chafing dish with low flame. Serve with party forks as wooden toothpicks are not strong enough.

Artichoke Frittata

Can do ahead

Yield: 4 doz
Preparing: 15-20 min
Baking: 1 hr

3   6-oz jars marinated
     artichokes, drained and
     finely chopped
½   lb sharp cheese, grated
1   medium onion, chopped

4   eggs, lightly beaten
6   soda crackers, crumbled
dash hot sauce
salt and pepper to taste

Combine all ingredients. Pour into greased 8" square baking pan. Bake at 325° for 1 hour. Cut into 1 inch squares. Serve hot.

Avocado-Egg Mold with Caviar

Must do ahead

Serves: 25
Preparing: 1 hr

2   envelopes unflavored
     gelatin
½   cup cold water

Egg Layer
4   hard boiled eggs, chopped
½   cup mayonnaise
¼   cup parsley, chopped
1-2 green onions, minced
salt and pepper to taste
hot sauce to taste

Sour Cream and Onion Layer
1   cup sour cream
3   Tb onion, minced
salt and pepper to taste

Avocado Layer
1   medium avocado, chopped
1   medium avocado, pureed
2   Tb lemon juice
2   Tb mayonnaise
salt and pepper to taste
hot sauce to taste

Topping
1   3-4 oz jar caviar, black or
     red
lemon juice to taste
2 oz pimento strips (optional)
sour cream (optional)

Line bottom and sides of a 1 quart soufflé dish or charlotte mold with foil or plastic wrap. Extend both ends of foil 4 inches beyond rim. Oil lightly. In a measuring cup, soften gelatin in cold water then dissolve gelatin by setting cup in a pan of hot water. Set aside.

Egg Layer: Combine chopped eggs, mayonnaise, parsley, onion, salt, pepper and hot sauce with 2 tablespoons gelatin mixture. Spread on bottom of pan.

Avocado Layer: Combine the avocados, lemon juice, mayonnaise, salt, pepper and hot sauce with 2 tablespoons gelatin. Spoon over egg layer.

Sour Cream-Onion Layer: Combine sour cream, onions, salt, pepper and 3 tablespoons gelatin mixture. Spoon over avocado layer.

Cover tightly with plastic wrap and refrigerate overnight.

Topping: At serving time, rinse caviar gently in fine sieve under cold running water. Sprinkle with lemon juice and drain well on paper towels. Invert mold onto serving platter. Remove foil or plastic wrap. Top with caviar, creating an attractive design using the pimento strips or additional sour cream. Serve with melba toast or mild crackers.

Avocado Dip

Must do ahead

Yield: 3-4 cups
Preparing: 10 min
Baking: 10 min

1	ripe avocado, peeled and chopped	8	oz Monterey Jack cheese, grated
1	8-oz carton sour cream		corn chips
1	4-oz can green chilies, chopped		

Place avocados on bottom of 1 quart ovenproof serving dish. Spread with sour cream and cover with green chiles. Cover with grated Monterey Jack cheese. Chill overnight. Warm in a 325° oven for about 10 minutes or until heated through. Serve with corn chips.

Guacamole

Must do ahead

Yield: 2 cups
Preparing: 15 min

2	avocados, peeled and pitted (save 1 pit)	1	Tb lemon juice
1	medium onion, finely chopped	1	tsp salt
1	4-oz can green chili peppers, chopped	½	tsp black pepper
		1	medium tomato, peeled, seeded and finely chopped
			corn chips

Puree avocados. Add onion, chili peppers, lemon juice, salt and pepper. Combine until well mixed. Fold in tomato. Put avocado pit in center to keep guacamole from turning dark. Cover and chill. Stir gently before serving, removing the pit. Serve with corn chips.

Broccoli Florets with Lime Dip

Must do ahead

Serves: 25
Preparing: 25 min

Lime Dip

2	cups sour cream
2	cups mayonnaise
½	cup fresh lime juice
1	Tb (scant) horseradish
1	Tb zest of lime
2	tsp Dijon mustard
1	tsp salt

6	bunches broccoli, cut into florets
½	to 1 cup Italian salad dressing
	lime slices

Combine ingredients for lime dip. Refrigerate overnight. Cut broccoli into florets with 2-3 inch stems. Steam prepared broccoli 1-3 minutes until color is bright green. Remove quickly and immerse in ice water. Drain well and chill. To serve, sprinkle broccoli lightly with Italian dressing. Arrange broccoli on a platter around small bowl of lime dip. Garnish with additional twisted lime slices.

Carrot Nibblers

Must do ahead

Serves: 10
Preparing: 25-30 min

1	lb carrots, peeled
3	cloves garlic, minced
2	Tb onion, coarsely chopped
3	Tb olive oil
¼	cup vinegar

1½	tsp salt
½	tsp dry mustard
1	Tb pickling spices in cheesecloth
⅛	tsp pepper, freshly ground
1	small onion, thinly sliced

Cut carrots into thin strips. Sauté garlic and onion in the olive oil until tender, about 5 minutes. Stir in vinegar, salt, mustard, pickling spices, pepper and carrots. Simmer covered for 5 minutes. Remove cheesecloth. Transfer carrot mixture to shallow dish. Top with layer of thinly sliced onions and refrigerate until needed, basting occasionally. Serve cold.

Bacon Stuffed Mushrooms

Serve immediately
Can partially do ahead

Yield: 32
Preparing: 20 min
Baking: 15-20 min

32	medium to large mushrooms
¼	cup butter, melted
12	slices bacon, cooked, drained, crumbled

¾	cup mayonnaise
1	medium onion, chopped
1½	cups sharp cheddar cheese, grated
	salt to season

Clean mushrooms and remove stems. Brush caps with butter. Combine bacon, mayonnaise, onion, cheese and salt. Fill mushroom caps with mixture. Place on baking sheet. Bake 15-20 minutes at 325° until cheese bubbles.

Cheese and Seafood Stuffed Mushrooms

Serve immediately
Can partially do ahead

Yield: 24
Preparing: 30 min
Baking: 10-15 min

24	large mushroom caps
¼	cup butter, melted
1	8-oz pkg cream cheese, softened
2	Tb sour cream
1	green onion, chopped

¼	cup Swiss cheese, grated
4	oz crabmeat or shrimp or a combination
	salt
	pepper
1	clove garlic, minced

Brush mushroom caps with butter and arrange on cookie sheet. Bake for 2-3 minutes at 375°. Beat cream cheese and sour cream together. Add remaining ingredients. Fill mushroom caps with mixture. Bake 10-15 minutes until hot and cheese bubbles.

Deviled Mushrooms

Serve immediately   Yield: 40
Can partially do ahead   Preparing: 30 min
Baking: 10-15 min

1	lb fresh mushrooms	2	tsp Dijon mustard
2	Tb butter		dried bread crumbs
1	4½-oz can deviled ham		Parmesan cheese

Remove stems from mushrooms. Chop the stems finely. Sauté in butter. Add deviled ham, mustard and enough bread crumbs to hold together. Stuff mushrooms. Sprinkle with Parmesan cheese. Bake at 375° for 10-15 minutes until hot.

Can add finely chopped onion and green pepper.

Florentine Mushrooms

Serve immediately   Yield: 24
Can partially do ahead   Preparing: 15 min
Baking: 15-18 min

1	12-oz pkg frozen spinach souffle, thawed	½	tsp salt
1	cup dry bread crumbs		melted butter
2	tsp lemon juice	24	large mushroom caps,
1	tsp instant minced onion		stems removed
			Parmesan cheese

Combine spinach souffle, bread crumbs, lemon juice, onion and salt. Brush caps with butter. Stuff mushroom caps with souffle mixture. Place on cookie sheet. Sprinkle with Parmesan cheese and bake at 375° for 15-18 minutes. Serve hot.

Monterey Stuffed Mushrooms

Serve immediately
Can partially do ahead

Yield: 40
Preparing: 15 min
Baking: 5-10 min

1   **lb fresh mushroom caps**
4   **oz Monterey jalapeño**
    cheese

Clean mushroom caps and remove stems. Fill with chunks of Monterey jalapeño cheese. Bake at 350° for 5-10 minutes until cheese melts.

Mushrooms Stuffed with Oysters

Serve immediately
Can partially do ahead

Yield: 40
Preparing: 15 min
Baking: 20 min

1   **lb fresh mushrooms**
6   **Tb butter**
1   **small clove garlic, minced**

juice of ½ lemon
½   **lb oysters, fresh**

Wash mushrooms. Remove stems. In a large skillet, saute mushroom caps and stems in 3 Tb of butter. Transfer caps to jelly roll pan. Set aside. In the same skillet with the mushroom stems combine remaining butter with garlic and lemon juice. Stir, scraping pan for 3 minutes. Put 1 fresh oyster in each mushroom cap. Pour butter sauce over cap (discard the stems). Sprinkle with salt. Bake at 350° for approximately 20 minutes until edges of oyster curl.

Sausage Stuffed Mushrooms

Serve immediately
Can partially do ahead

Yield: 30
Preparing: 45 min
Baking: 10 min

30 mushroom caps	½ cup dry bread crumbs
¼ cup butter, melted	1 Tb pecans, minced
½ lb bulk sausage	3 Tb fresh parsley, minced
1 medium onion, minced	½ tsp thyme
mushroom stems, minced	2 Tb heavy cream
¼ cup Madeira or sherry	

Remove mushroom stems and chop. Brush caps with butter. In a skillet, sauté sausage and onion. Drain fat, return mixture to pan. Add mushroom stems and Madeira. Increase heat and cook until liquid has evaporated. Add remaining ingredients. Fill mushroom caps. Bake at 350° for 10 minutes or broil until brown on top.

Hot Stuffed Mushrooms

Serve immediately
Can partially do ahead

Yield: 12
Preparing: 30 min
Baking: 15 min

12 fresh mushrooms	1 egg, beaten
4 Tb butter	dash salt
1 clove garlic, crushed	pepper
4 oz lobster or crabmeat	bread crumbs
½ tsp Worcestershire sauce	

Clean mushrooms. Remove stems and chop. Brush with melted butter. Sauté stems and garlic in butter. Transfer to small bowl. Add lobster or crabmeat, Worcestershire sauce, egg, salt and pepper. Stir to combine. Fill caps with mixture. Sprinkle bread crumbs on top. Top with melted butter. Bake in 350° oven for 15 minutes.

New Year's Day Dip

Can do ahead

Yield: 3 cups
Preparing: 1 hr
Cooking: 30 min

¼	cup green pepper, finely chopped	¼	tsp nutmeg
4	jalapeño peppers, finely chopped	¼	tsp cinnamon
2	celery ribs, finely chopped	2	16-oz cans black-eyed peas
1	large onion, minced	1	14-oz can whole tomatoes, drained and chopped
1	tsp hot sauce		
½	cup catsup	1	tsp garlic powder
1	tsp salt	½	cup bacon drippings
1	tsp coarsely ground pepper	3	Tb flour
3	chicken bouillon cubes		tortilla chips

In a large saucepan, combine the first eleven ingredients. Bring to a simmer over low heat. Add black-eyed peas, tomatoes and garlic. Cook for 30 minutes. Blend bacon drippings with flour in a small bowl. Stir into peas and simmer for 10 minutes. Serve in a chafing dish with tortilla chips.

Vidalia Onion Spread

Must do ahead

Yield: 3 cups
Preparing: 10 min

6	medium Vidalia onions	½	cup mayonnaise
½	cup cider vinegar	1	tsp celery salt
1	cup sugar		melba rounds
2	cups water		

Slice onions very thin. Combine with vinegar, sugar and water. Let stand in refrigerator three to four hours. Drain liquid from onions thoroughly. Combine marinated onions with mayonnaise and celery salt. Serve with melba rounds.

Stuffed Snow Peas

Must do ahead

Yield: 24
Preparing: 1 hr

2	**dozen fresh snow peas**
¾	**cup cream cheese, softened, whipped**
2	**Tb orange juice**

1½	**tsp horseradish**
⅛	**tsp pepper, freshly ground**
	grated orange rind

Trim ends from snow peas. Place peas in a steaming basket. Plunge basket into boiling water and remove immediately. Place snow peas in bowl of ice water and refrigerate. Combine cream cheese, orange juice, horseradish and pepper. Stir until smooth. Chill for 1 hour. Use a sharp knife to carefully slit one side of each pea pod. Spoon cream cheese mixture into decorating bag fitted with decorative tip. Pipe approximately 1½ teaspoon mixture in each pea pod. Sprinkle with grated orange rind. Refrigerate until ready to serve.

Reverse Potato Skins

Can partially do ahead

Yield: 16 pieces
Preparing: 25 min

1	**cup sour cream**
2	**green onions, chopped**
1	**cup cheddar cheese, grated**
4	**slices bacon, fried and crumbled**

½	**cup fresh mushrooms, sliced and sautéed**
	salt
2	**medium baking potatoes, baked**
	oil

Combine first six ingredients to make dip. Cut each potato into eight wedges, leaving on skins. Deep fry for 1-2 minutes until golden. Drain well. Arrange wedges on platter surrounding dip. Serve hot.

Stuffed Potato Shells

Can partially do ahead

Yield: 8 pieces
Preparing: 30 min
Cooking: microwave
2½-4 min

2	baking potatoes (5 to 7 oz each)	¼	cup sour cream
4	slices bacon	½	cup cheddar cheese, grated
¼	tsp salt	1	Tb green onion, chopped
⅛	tsp pepper		

Microwave pierced potatoes 5-7½ minutes, turning after half the time. Let stand 5 minutes. Place bacon between paper towels. Microwave 1-2 minutes on high. Crumble and set aside. Slice each potato in half lengthwise then crosswise. Carefully scoop out centers leaving ¼ inch potato next to skin. Arrange skins on serving plate. Sprinkle with salt and pepper. Spread thin layer of sour cream in each shell. Sprinkle with cheese, green onion and crumbled bacon. Microwave on 50% for 2½-4 minutes until cheese melts, rotating plate after half the cooking time. May cut each piece one more time to serve 16.

Hot Spinach Dip

Can partially do ahead

Yield: 2½ cups
Preparing: 15 min
Cooking: 15 min

1	10-oz pkg frozen chopped spinach	8	slices of bacon, cooked and crumbled
1	8-oz pkg cream cheese, softened	2	green onions, chopped
½	cup mayonnaise	⅓	cup Parmesan cheese, grated
		2	tsp lemon juice

Cook spinach according to directions on package. Cool. Remove all moisture by squeezing with paper towels. Add cream cheese, mayonnaise, bacon, onions, cheese and lemon juice. Heat in conventional oven at 350° for 15 minutes or in microwave at 70% for 3 minutes. Serve with fresh vegetables or crackers.

Spinach-Feta Triangles

Serve immediately
Can freeze

Yield: 60
Preparing: 1 hr
Baking: 25 min

2	10-oz pkgs frozen, chopped spinach, thawed	⅓	cup ricotta cheese
½	cup onion, finely chopped	¼	cup feta cheese, crumbled
3	Tb olive oil	1	lb phyllo pastry, thawed*
	nutmeg, salt and pepper to taste	½	lb butter, melted
3	Tb dried dill		

Filling: Drain thawed spinach and squeeze dry. Sauté onion in olive oil until soft and golden. Add spinach and cook over low heat, stirring frequently, until mixture is dry. Season with nutmeg, salt and pepper. Add dill. Cool completely. Add ricotta cheese, then feta cheese. Taste and correct seasoning.

Assembling triangles: Place one sheet of phyllo on flat surface and brush with butter. Top with second sheet and butter again. Cover unused phyllo with damp towel until ready to use. Cut the buttered phyllo sheets crosswise into fifths. Place rounded teaspoon of filling about an inch from the end of the first strip. Form a triangle by folding right-hand corner across filling to opposite side. Continue folding, as if folding a flag, until the strip is used. Do not fold too tightly as filling will expand with baking. Place stuffed triangle seam-side down on a buttered baking sheet. Brush top with butter. Continue with remaining phyllo dough.

Filled phyllo triangles can be kept in refrigerator, unbaked, for 24 hours or frozen immediately. If freezing, place on unbuttered baking sheet, freeze overnight and transfer to plastic bag until needed.

Bake freshly made triangles in upper third of 350° oven for about 25 minutes. Bake frozen triangles, unthawed, on a buttered baking sheet at 350° for 45 minutes or until filling is hot. Serve immediately.

*Defrost phyllo pastry in its original wrapper in the refrigerator for at least two days.

Cherry Bombs

Can do ahead

Serves: 6-8
Preparing: 10 min

1	tsp Beau Monde (Spice Islands)	1	tsp seasoned salt
1	tsp dill	1	pint cherry tomatoes

Combine Beau Monde, dill and seasoned salt in small plastic bag. Rinse tomatoes. Place 3-5 tomatoes in bag and shake. Remove. Repeat until all tomatoes are coated.

Salsa Cruda

Can do ahead

Yield: 3 cups
Preparing: 10 min

6	medium ripe tomatoes, peeled and chopped	1	tsp salt
½	cup canned green chilies, diced	1-3	canned jalapeño peppers, diced
⅓	cup onion, minced		corn chips

Combine all ingredients except corn chips. Serve with corn chips.

Marinated Vegetable Medley

Must do ahead

Choose any five of the following:

1	can green beans, drained		2	cups cucumber, sliced
1	can asparagus, drained		2	cups (1 small head) cauliflower
1	can carrots, drained			
1	can artichoke hearts, drained		2	cups (1 bunch) broccoli florets
2	cups (½ lb) fresh mushrooms, cleaned		2	medium green peppers, sliced
2	cups cherry tomatoes		1	small red onion, sliced and separated into rings
2	cups raw squash, sliced			

Marinade

1	cup vegetable oil		1	Tb dried Italian seasoning
½	cup white wine vinegar		2	tsp dry mustard
½	cup sugar		1	tsp salt

Combine your choice of vegetables in a large mixing bowl or storage container. Combine marinade ingredients and pour over vegetables and toss. Cover. Chill overnight. Drain and arrange on platter for serving.

Zucchini Squares

Can do ahead
Can freeze

Yield: 4-5 doz
Preparing: 20 min
Baking: 25-30

4	eggs, beaten	2	Tb parsley, chopped
½	cup vegetable oil	¼	tsp salt
1	cup Bisquick	½	tsp seasoned salt
3	cups zucchini, unpeeled and sliced	½	tsp oregano
		⅛	tsp pepper, freshly ground
½	cup onion, finely chopped	1	clove garlic, minced (optional)
½	cup Parmesan cheese, grated		dash of hot sauce (optional)

Preheat oven to 350° and grease 9″ × 13″ pan. Combine eggs, oil and Bisquick. Add remaining ingredients and spread into pan. Bake 25-30 minutes or until brown. Cut into bite size squares. Serve warm or cold. *Substitute 3 cups other vegetables (green tomatoes, carrots, yellow squash, etc.)*

Chunky Vegetable Dip

Must do ahead

Yield: 3 cups
Preparing: 20 min

1	10-oz pkg frozen spinach, chopped	1	cup sour cream
1	1⅝ oz pkg Knorr's Vegetable Soup Mix	1	medium onion or less, chopped
1	cup mayonnaise	1	8-oz can water chestnuts, drained and chopped

Thaw spinach. Squeeze to remove moisture. Combine with remaining ingredients and mix well. Cover and chill. Serve with vegetables or crackers.

Herb Curry Dip

Must do ahead

Yield: 1½ cups
Preparing: 15 min

1	cup mayonnaise		1	Tb onion, grated
½	cup sour cream		1½	tsp lemon juice
1	tsp salad herbs, crushed		½	tsp Worcestershire sauce
¼	tsp salt		2	tsp capers, drained
⅛	tsp curry powder			(optional)
1	Tb parsley, snipped			vegetables

Combine all ingredients and chill. For full flavor, refrigerate overnight. Serve with fresh vegetables.

Louisiana Dip

Must do ahead

Yield: 3 cups
Preparing: 15 min

16	oz carton sour cream			juice of 1 lemon
1	pkg Italian salad dressing mix		1	avocado, finely chopped
			1	tomato, finely chopped
2	Tb mayonnaise			dash of hot sauce

Combine all ingredients. Chill well. Serve with chips or raw vegetables.

Raspberry Dip

Can do ahead

Yield: 2 cups
Preparing: 30 min

¼   cup shredded coconut
2   Tb pecans, finely chopped
1   cup sour cream
¼-½ cup raspberry preserves
2   Tb milk

fresh fruit (apple, orange and
   pear wedges, banana
   pieces, strawberries,
   grapes, melon balls)
lemon juice

Combine coconut, pecans, sour cream, preserves and milk. Toss apple, pear and banana pieces in lemon juice. Arrange fruit around a bowl of the dip. Serve chilled.

Macaroon Fruit Dip

Must do ahead

Yield: 3 cups
Preparing: 5 min

12 macaroons, crushed
¼   cup brown sugar, packed

1   pint sour cream
fresh fruit

Mix all ingredients and chill several hours to soften macaroons. Do not stir again. Serve with strawberries, melon, bananas, grapes and pineapple.

Fruit Spread

Can do ahead

Yield: 3 cups
Preparing: 10 min

1   17-oz can fruit cocktail,
    drained
1   8-oz pkg cream cheese
2   Tb mayonnaise

2   Tb green onion, chopped
3-4 Tb bacon bits
fruit

In a small bowl, mash fruit cocktail. Set aside. Beat cream cheese with mayonnaise until soft and smooth. Add fruit cocktail and onion to cheese mixture, beating to combine. Add bacon bits and allow to stand in covered bowl in refrigerator for 30 minutes before serving. Use as a spread for sliced apples, pears or fresh pineapple.

New Jezebel Sauce

Must do ahead

Yield: 2 cups
Preparing: 5 min

1   9-oz jar apricot or apricot-
    pineapple preserves
1   9-oz jar apple jelly
2½ oz horseradish

2   Tb dry mustard
½   tsp cracked black pepper
1   8-oz pkg cream cheese

Combine all ingredients except cream cheese. Chill. To serve, pour sauce over cream cheese. Surround with bland crackers.

Apricot Cheese Dip

Can do ahead

Yield: 1⅓ cups
Preparing: 20 min

½   **cup dried apricots**
1   **Tb sugar**
1   **3-oz pkg cream cheese, cubed**

½   **cup sour cream**
⅛   **tsp ground nutmeg**
fresh fruit

Simmer apricots in 1 cup water, covered, for 15 minutes or until tender. Drain, reserving ¼ cup liquid. Combine apricots, the reserved liquid and sugar in a blender or processor and blend until smooth. Add cheese, sour cream and nutmeg. Blend until smooth. Transfer to a serving dish, cover and chill until ready to use. Serve with fresh fruit.

Pineapple-Date Dip for Apples

Must do ahead

Yield: 2 cups
Preparing: 30 min

1   **8 oz pkg cream cheese, softened**
1   **Tb mayonnaise**
1   **7 oz can crushed pineap-ple, drained**

1   **cup dates, chopped**
½   **cup pecans, chopped**
Granny Smith apples
1   **6 oz can frozen lemonade concentrate, thawed**

To prepare dip, beat cream cheese and mayonnaise together until smooth. Stir in crushed pineapple, dates, and pecans. Cover and refrigerate up to two days. Prior to serving, core and slice apples but do not peel. Drop slices in thawed concentrate for 5-10 minutes. Drain. Spread pineapple-date dip on each wedge and arrange on tray.

Tangy Orange Cheese

Must do ahead

Yield: 2½ cups
Preparing: 15 min

2   8-oz pkgs cream cheese, softened
½   cup powdered sugar
2   Tb orange peel, grated
2   Tb Cointreau

2   Tb frozen orange juice concentrate, undiluted
Swedish gingersnaps
fruit

In a large bowl, combine cream cheese, sugar, orange peel, Cointreau and orange juice concentrate. Blend thoroughly. Cover tightly and refrigerate overnight. Serve at room temperature as a spread for gingersnaps, slices of fruit (apples, pears, tangerines, banana spears) or dessert breads (banana, date nut). If necessary, thin mixture with additional orange juice. *Grand Marnier makes a sweeter version.*

Brandied Raisin Mold

Must do ahead

Yield: 4 cups
Preparing: 30 min

1   cup golden raisins
brandy to cover
12   oz cream cheese, softened
½   cup butter, softened
½   cup sour cream
½   cup sugar

1   envelope gelatin
¼   cup cold water
1   cup almonds, slivered
2   lemons, grated rind
strawberries

Soak raisins overnight in enough brandy to cover. Drain and blot dry. Combine cream cheese, butter, sour cream and sugar. Dissolve gelatin in cold water over hot water in a double boiler. Combine with cream cheese mixture. Add almonds, lemon rind and raisins. Pour into a greased 1 quart mold. Chill. Garnish with fresh strawberries. Serve with crackers.

Melon and Avocado with Prosciutto

Must do ahead

Yield: 40
Preparing: 30 min.

1	large cantaloupe	1	cup French dressing
1	large avocado	½	lb prosciutto, thinly sliced
¼	cup lemon juice		

Peel cantaloupe and avocado and cut into bite size pieces. Sprinkle with lemon juice and then marinate in French dressing for 1 hour. Wrap each piece of fruit with strips of prosciutto and secure with wooden picks.

Glorified Grapes

Must do ahead

Yield: 100
Preparing: 1 hr

¾	lb seedless grapes, red or green	2	oz Roquefort cheese, softened
¾	lb (shelled) almonds, pecans or walnuts	2	Tb heavy cream
1	8-oz pkg cream cheese, softened		

Wash and dry grapes. Preheat oven to 275°. Spread nuts on cookie sheet and bake until toasted. After nuts are cool, chop finely and spread on a platter. In a bowl, combine cheeses and heavy cream. Beat with mixer until smooth. Drop grapes into cheese mixture and gently stir to coat. Roll coated grapes in nuts and put on a tray lined with waxed paper until ready to serve. Cover well. Chill. Garnish serving tray with fresh mint sprigs.

N·U·T·S & N·I·B·B·L·E·S

Butterless Salted Pecans

Can do ahead

Yield: 8 cups
Preparing: 20 min
Cooking: 30 min

1	egg white	1	Tb salt or more to taste
8	cups pecan halves		

Beat egg white until stiff. Stir in nuts until well coated (the egg white will almost disappear). Add salt and toss well. Spread on 2 cookie sheets. Bake 30 minutes at 300°. Cool and store in airtight container.

Sherried Walnuts

Must do ahead

Yield: 6 cups
Preparing: 30 min

¼	cup dry sherry	2	Tb light corn syrup
1½	cups brown sugar	4-6	cups walnut halves
¼	tsp salt	½	cup granulated sugar
1	Tb pumpkin pie spice		

Combine first 5 ingredients. Add walnuts, stir to coat. Place in ziplock bag, add granulated sugar and shake to lightly coat. Remove from bag and dry overnight on waxed paper. Store in airtight container.

Nutty Raisin Party Mix

Can do ahead

2	6-oz cans whole almonds	6	Tb margarine, melted
1	8-oz jar dry roasted pea-nuts	1½	Tb soy sauce
1	7-oz jar dry roasted ca-shews	1½	Tb Worcestershire sauce
1	5-oz can chow mein noo-dles	3	dashes hot sauce
		1	15-oz pkg raisins

Combine nuts and noodles in large bowl. Blend margarine and sauces and pour over nuts, tossing to coat. Spread half of the mixture on a jelly roll pan. Bake in 325° oven for 15 minutes. Cool completely. Repeat the process with the remaining mixture. Put all the mixture in a large container and add raisins, mixing well. Store in airtight container.

Barbecued Nuts

Can do ahead

¼	cup butter	⅛	tsp cayenne pepper (optional)
¼	cup A-1 Steak Sauce	3	cups nuts (pecans, unsalted peanuts, walnuts, etc.)
2	tsp celery salt		

Melt butter. Add A-1 Steak Sauce, celery salt and cayenne pepper. Heat thoroughly and then pour over nuts, mixing well. Spread nuts on ungreased cookie sheet and bake in 350° oven for 20 minutes, stirring once. Drain nuts on paper towels until cool. Store in airtight container.

Sugared Peanuts

Must do ahead

Yield: 3 cups
Preparing: 15 min
Baking: 30 min

½   cup water
1   cup sugar

3   cups raw shelled peanuts
    with skins

Place all ingredients in an iron skillet. Stir over medium heat for 5-7 minutes or until nuts are completely coated and no longer sticky. Pour the nuts on a large cookie sheet in a single layer and bake in 275° oven for 30 minutes, shaking the pan several times. Cool at least 2 hours before serving. Keeps indefinitely in an airtight container.

P-Nut Sticks

Can do ahead

Yield: 50
Preparing: 45 min

8-9 bread slices
1   cup creamy peanut butter
⅓   cup oil

2   cups fresh bread crumbs
⅓   cup sesame seeds or
    finely chopped peanuts

Cut crusts from bread slices. Cut each slice into 6 strips. Toast on cookie sheet in a 300-325° oven until brown and crisp. Combine peanut butter and oil in a double boiler and melt. In a small bowl, combine bread crumbs and sesame seeds (or peanuts). Dip bread sticks into peanut butter mixture and then into bread crumbs. Put on brown paper to cool. Store in airtight container.

Orange Glazed Pecans

Can do ahead

Yield: 2-3 cups
Preparing: 10 min
Cooking: 8 min

1 cup sugar **juice of one orange**	**2½ cups pecan halves**

Combine sugar and orange juice in saucepan. Cook on medium heat for about 2 minutes until a syrup forms. Add pecans and stir constantly for 3-5 minutes until the syrup is absorbed. Pour nuts on waxed paper to cool.

Party Snacks

Can partially do ahead

Yield: 36
Preparing: 15 min

6 oz cheddar cheese, grated **1 2.8-oz can onion rings,** ** coarsely crumbled**	**½ cup mayonnaise (may need** ** more)** **1 loaf cocktail rye**

Combine cheese, onion rings and mayonnaise together. Spread on cocktail rye. Broil until bubbly.

Zesty Nibbles

Must do ahead

Yield: 8 cups
Preparing: 5 min

2 16-oz boxes oyster ** crackers** **1 cup vegetable oil** **1 1-oz pkg buttermilk salad** ** dressing mix**	**1 tsp dill weed** **1 tsp lemon pepper** **½ tsp garlic powder**

Place crackers in large plastic container. Warm the oil. Add seasonings to the oil. Pour mixture over crackers and toss gently. Cover tightly and let stand for 24 hours. *Can substitute blue cheese salad dressing mix.*

Popcorn Potpourri

Can do ahead

Yield: 2½ qts
Preparing: 10 min
Baking: 10 min

2	qts freshly popped pop-corn, unsalted	¼	cup butter or margarine, melted
1	6¼-oz can cashew nuts	1½	Tb soy sauce
1	5-oz can chow mein noodles	¾	tsp ground ginger

Combine popcorn, cashews and noodles. Stir butter, soy sauce and ginger until well blended. Pour over popcorn mixture and toss well. Transfer to a jelly roll pan and bake at 350° for 5 to 10 minutes. Serve or store in an airtight container.

Herb Rolls

Can partially do ahead

Yield: 40
Preparing: 15 min
Baking: 10-15 min

Herb Mix

¼	cup parsley flakes	¼	cup butter, melted
2	Tb onion flakes	3	Tb Herb Mix
4	tsp dill seed	1	10-count can refrigerated biscuits
½	cup Parmesan cheese, grated		

pinch dill weed
pinch sweet basil
⅛ tsp garlic salt

Combine ingredients for Herb Mix and set aside. Combine butter and 3 tablespoons of Herb Mix. Cut biscuits into quarters and dip into mixture. Bake on jelly roll pan for 10-15 minutes at 400°. Serve immediately. Store remaining Herb Mix in refrigerator. *Herb Mix is also good added to sour cream for potatoes or with other vegetables.*

Blue Cheese Wafers

Can do ahead
Can freeze

Yield: 3 dozen
Preparing: 15 min
Baking: 10 min

6 oz cheddar cheese, grated	**1** cup butter, softened
3 oz blue cheese, crumbled	**1½** tsp seasoned salt
dash cayenne	**1** cup pecans, chopped
2⅔ cups flour	

With a mixer, combine all ingredients adding the pecans last. Shape the dough into a long roll about 1½" in diameter. Wrap the roll in wax paper and refrigerate until the roll is well chilled. Slice ⅛-¼ inch thick. Make a cross-hatch pattern with the tines of a fork. Bake at 375° for 10 minutes. May be frozen or stored in an airtight container.

Puff Pastry Straws

Can partially do ahead

Yield: 5 dozen
Preparing: 30 min
Baking: 8-10 min

1 lb puff pastry (Pepperidge Farm)
½ cup poppy or sesame seeds

Preheat oven to 400°. Work with one sheet of pastry at a time. Cover and refrigerate the other sheet. Roll the sheet into a rectangle ⅛" thick. Sprinkle seeds onto pastry and press in with rolling pin. Cut each sheet into thirds and cut each third into ½" strips. Twist strips and place on baking sheet that has been sprayed with water. Bake 8-10 minutes until golden brown. Best when served immediately. *Also good with Parmesan or grated cheddar cheese.*

Wassail

Can do ahead

Yield: 1½ gallons
Preparing: 20 min

1	gallon apple cider	1	cup sugar
1	quart orange juice	24	whole cloves
1	quart pineapple juice	4	cinnamon sticks
8	oz lemon juice		Cheesecloth

Bring cider, juices, and sugar to a boil. Tie spices in cheesecloth. Reduce heat, add spices, and steep for 10 minutes. Strain before serving.

Apricot Spiced Punch

Must do ahead

Yield: 1½ - 2 qts
Preparing: 10 min
Cooking: 5 min

3	cups apricot nectar	3	Tb lemon juice
3	cups apple cider	8	whole cloves
1	cup water	7	sticks cinnamon
3	Tb sugar		

In a 3 quart saucepan, combine first 6 ingredients. Bring to a boil, stirring until sugar dissolves. Remove from heat and let stand 2 hours. Reheat before serving. Serve in mugs with cinnamon sticks.

Fruit Slush

Must do ahead
Can freeze

Yield: 1 gallon
Preparing: 30 min

6   bananas
1½ cup sugar
1   29-oz can apricots,
     chopped
1   20-oz can crushed pineap-
     ple

2   6-oz cans frozen orange
     juice
2   juice cans of water
juice of 3 lemons
2-4 28-oz bottles ginger ale

Mash bananas and add sugar. Puree apricots and pineapple. Add orange juice, water, and lemon juice. Mix and freeze in a large covered container. It may take up to one day to freeze. To serve, fill cups half way with fruit mixture. Add ginger ale to fill glass. Mixture may be softened in a punch bowl and then ginger ale poured over mixture immediately before serving. *Can serve frozen mixture as sherbet.*

Citrus Cooler

Must do ahead
Can freeze

Yield: 5½ qts
Preparing: 10 min
Cooking: 5 min

1½-2 cups sugar
2½ cups water
1   46-oz can pineapple juice
1   46-oz can orange juice

1½ cups lemon juice
1½ qts ginger ale or
champagne
pineapple wedges
orange wedges

Combine sugar and water in saucepan. Bring to a boil, stirring until sugar dissolves. Pour mixture into 4½ quart freezer container. Stir in fruit juices. Freeze until firm. Remove from freezer 1½-2 hours before serving. Mixture should be slushy. Stir in ginger ale or champagne. Garnish with pineapple and orange wedges.

Bloody Mary

Must do ahead

Yield: 1½ qts
Preparing: 10 min

1	32-oz bottle Clamato juice	5	Tb Worcestershire sauce
5	oz vodka		celery salt
2	Tb lime juice		

Mix first four ingredients. Sprinkle generously with celery salt and refrigerate overnight. Serve in tall glasses with celery stalks as garnish.

Pimm's Cup

Serve immediately

Yield: 1 serving

1½	oz Pimm's #1		7-Up
1	slice lemon		Cucumber Spear

Pour Pimm's over ice in tall glass. Add lemon slice. Fill with 7-Up and garnish with cucumber spear.

Whispers

Serve immediately

Yield: ½ gallon
Preparing: 5 min

½	gallon coffee ice cream	6	Tb Kahlua
6	Tb brandy		whipped cream (optional)

Combine ice cream, brandy and Kahlua in blender. *To serve, top with whipped cream if desired.*

White Sangria

Must do ahead

Yield: 1 gallon
Preparing: 20 min

1   lemon
1   orange
1   lime
1   gallon Chablis
sugar to taste

8-10 sprigs fresh mint
8-10 strawberries
soda water or lemon-lime soft
    drink (optional)

Juice and then quarter lemon, orange, and lime. Combine Chablis, fruit juices, quartered fruits, sugar, mint, and strawberries. Steep all day. Strain before serving. Dilute with soda water if serving to guests who desire a very diluted drink. Dilute with lemon-lime soft drink for those preferring a sweeter drink. Garnish with additional fresh mint or fruit if desired.

Strawberry Margaritas

Can freeze

Yield: 1 qt
Preparing: 10-15 min

16   oz frozen strawberries
4½   oz tequila
1½   oz triple sec
3   oz lime juice

ice, crushed
salt
limes

Puree strawberries in blender. Add tequila, triple sec, lime juice, and ice. Mix. Run wedge of lime around rim of stemmed glass. Dip in salt. Fill with margaritas. Garnish with lime slices.

Frozen Margaritas

Can do ahead
Can freeze

Yield: 1 qt
Preparing: 5 min

1	6-oz can frozen limeade concentrate, thawed	ice lemon slices
6	oz tequila	salt
2	oz triple sec	

Combine limeade, tequila, and triple sec in blender. Add ice to fill the blender. Blend until smooth. Store in freezer. To serve, rub a lemon slice around the rim of a stemmed glass and dip in salt. Fill with frozen mixture.

Kir Royale

Serve immediately

Yield: 3½ qts
Preparing: 10 min

2	10-oz packages frozen raspberries, thawed	1 cup creme de cassis, chilled
1	32-oz bottle club soda, chilled	3 750 ml bottles Champagne, chilled

Place one package of raspberries in a blender. Process until smooth. Strain. Pour raspberry puree into punch bowl with club soda and cassis. Stir gently. Break up remaining package of raspberries and add to punch bowl. Slowly pour Champagne around bowl stirring gently. Serve at once.

Cranberry Banger Punch

Must do ahead

Yield: 5 qts
Preparing: 15 min

1	12-oz can orange juice concentrate, thawed
3	cups water
½	cup orange liqueur
	cherries

2	qts cranberry juice cocktail, chilled
1	fifth vodka
1	32-oz bottle lemon-lime drink, chilled

Combine orange juice, water and orange liqueur. Pour into ice cube trays, place cherry in each cube. Freeze. Combine cranberry juice cocktail and vodka in punch bowl. Slowly pour lemon-lime drink down the side of punch bowl and stir. Float juice cubes in punch. *For non-alcoholic punch, vodka can be eliminated without altering taste.*

Whiskey Punch

Can partially do ahead

Yield: 6 qts
Preparing: 10 min

1	6-oz can lemonade concentrate, thawed
2	12-oz cans orange juice concentrate, thawed
1	46-oz can unsweetened pineapple juice

1	qt ginger ale
1	qt soda water
2	fifths bourbon
	orange slices or cherries

Dilute lemonade and orange juice as directed. Combine lemonade, orange juice and pineapple juice. Slowly add ginger ale, soda water and bourbon. Mix, add ice cubes and serve. Garnish with orange slices or cherries. *For non-alcoholic punch, omit bourbon and increase ginger ale and soda to 2 quarts each.*

Tom and Jerrys

Can do ahead

Yield: 2 qts mix
Preparing: 40 min

12	eggs, separated	1	fifth rum
2	cups granulated sugar	1	fifth bourbon
1	lb powdered sugar		nutmeg
1	can sweetened condensed milk		

Beat egg whites and gradually add granulated sugar. Add ½ pound of the powdered sugar and beat until smooth. To unbeaten egg yolks, add remaining ½ pound powdered sugar and condensed milk. Beat vigorously until well combined. Fold egg yolk mixture into egg white mixture. Combine rum and bourbon in a pitcher. Place 1-2 tablespoons of egg mixture in a mug. Add 1½ ounces of rum-bourbon mixture. Cover with boiling water. Stir. Top with nutmeg.

Hot Buttered Rum

Can freeze

Yield: 1 qt mix;
64 servings
Preparing: 15 min

1	cup butter, softened	1	pint vanilla ice cream, softened
½	lb light brown sugar		light rum
½	lb powdered sugar		boiling water
1	tsp cinnamon		
1	tsp nutmeg		

Cream butter with brown sugar, powdered sugar, cinnamon and nutmeg. Blend in ice cream. Cover and store in the freezer. When ready to use, put 1 tablespoon of mixture and 1½ oz of light rum into mug, fill with boiling water.

use 2 heaping tblsp. of mix to 2 oz. rum (big jigger) H. water —use 1¼ c.

PARTY PLANNING

A Sterling Affair

Tenderloin Cubes
Béarnaise Sauce

Crab Mornay

Cheese Squares Florentine

Broccoli Florets with Lime Dip

Apricot Brie Wrapped in Phyllo

Raspberry Dip for Fruit

Sherried Walnuts

Kir Royale

Mike and Carolyn Brown
cordially invite you to a
Cocktail Buffet
Saturday, the twenty-second of February
seven o'clock
200 Pine Avenue

R.s.v.p.
555-2106

A Sterling Affair

Had I the heavens' embroidered cloths,
Enwrought with gold and silver light.
— W.B. Yeats, "He Wishes for the Cloths of Heaven"

Let black, white, and the shimmer of silver set the scene for your Sterling Affair, a truly elegant evening. Against the crisp backdrop of a winter's night, the house is a fantasy of lights and mirrors. The guest list is for 100, the dress is formal, and since the hostess has prepared ahead, she will be at leisure to enjoy herself.

THE DECORATIONS: If you ever wanted to pull out all the stops on a party, this is your chance. Keep everything within your black, white, and silver theme, but don't skimp on the details.

Elegant doesn't always mean complicated — or expensive. Cover your serving table with a white tablecloth (pull out grandmother's damask no matter how much ironing it takes!) and add a runner of bevelled mirror squares. Scatter rock candy and clear glass pebbles across the mirror, light with votive candles, and you have the ultimate in dazzle. As a centerpiece, present the sculptural beauty of a single white amaryllis in a silver bowl. Decorate the bars as smaller versions of your serving table, with perhaps pink amaryllis instead of white for contrast.

Carry sparkle to every corner of the house with votive candles and strings of white miniature lights. Move some of your furniture out for the evening to make more space for your guests. Dim lighting, and the glow of candles will disguise the fact that your rooms are a little barer than usual.

PRESENTING THE FOOD: Beg, borrow, or rent silver serving dishes for your Sterling Affair! Silver trays and chafing dishes will quietly underscore the elegance of the occasion.

Elegant, well-prepared food deserves to be well presented. For the BEEF TENDERLOIN, cover a silver platter with red-tipped lettuce and create a fan with the meat beginning at an upper corner of the platter. Garnish the beginning point of the fan with a tomato rose resting on leaves of acuba or some other small-leafed evergreen from the yard. Serve the BÉARNAISE SAUCE in a scooped-out acorn squash, and don't forget toothpicks and waste bowls on either side of the platter.

While the BEEF TENDERLOIN dominates one end of the table, the CRAB MORNAY is the center of attention at the other. Rest a silver chafing dish (equipped with long-handled iced teaspoons) on a silver platter, and place a circle of crackers around the base of the dish.

The BROCCOLI AND LIME DIP will be especially inviting when served from a grapefruit shell, scooped out and scalloped. Surround the shell with broccoli florets, and garnish with thin lime slices.

OTHER TOUCHES:

• An "English butler" (perhaps an out-of-work actor or a college student) in proper attire could provide both an extra pair of hands and a touch of theatre to your Sterling Affair.

• Don't forget that the hostess is part of the "decoration" for a formal affair. When the party is designed around a color scheme, dress yourself either in keeping with the theme, or in deliberate stunning contrast.

• Miniature lights are available in battery-powered versions. Use these portable strings on your table as an addition to votive candles for extra sparkle.

A Sterling Affair
Serves 100 Guests

Timetable	Recipe	# of Recipes	Storage
2 Weeks Ahead	Sherried Walnuts	2	C
	Cheese Squares Florentine — prepare	4	F
1 Day Ahead	Raspberry Dip for Fruit — prepare the dip	3	R
	Broccoli Florets with Lime Dip — prepare the dip	2	R
	Crab Mornay — prepare dip except for crabmeat	1	R
Morning of Party	Tenderloin Cubes Béarnaise Sauce	20 lbs 2	R R
	Raspberry Dip for Fruit — prepare fresh fruit	1½ gallons	R
	Apricot Brie Wrapped in Phyllo — assemble	2	R
Afternoon of Party	Broccoli Florets with Lime Dip — prepare broccoli		R
	Tenderloin Cubes — remove from refrigerator 1½ hours before serving		
Serving Time	Apricot Brie Wrapped in Phyllo — bake		
	Crab Mornay — add crabmeat and heat		
	Cheese Squares Florentine — heat		
	Kir Royale	8	

C = airtight container
F = freezer
R = refrigerator

Beef Tenderloin with Béarnaise

English Garden Party

Chicken Almond Puffs

Velvet Crab   Shrimp Taiwan

Ham Roll-Ups

Avocado Egg Mold with Caviar

Stuffed Snow Peas

Pineapple-Date Dip for Apples

Cream Cheese Pinwheels

Puff Pastry Straws

Orange Glazed Pecans

Citrus Cooler   Pimm's Cup

English Garden Party

honoring

David and Julie Taylor

Saturday, the eleventh of May

four to six o'clock

1000 Magnolia Street

Regrets:
Steve and Cathy Allen 555-3210

English Garden Party

All that in this delightful garden grows,
Should happy be, and have immortal bliss.
— Edmund Spenser, "The Faerie Queen"

The simple mention of a garden party evokes romantic visions of another place and time: women in picture hats, handsome men striking croquet balls across a smooth lawn, and chintz, china, and gleaming silver everywhere. A garden party, especially in the first warm days of spring or early summer when most yards are at their best, is the perfect setting for a late Sunday afternoon party. The English Garden Party can also easily be adapted for special events, such as a christening or bridal shower, or any other occasion that calls for a touch of romance.

DECORATIONS: Cover your tables with white tablecloths (damask if you have it, but sheets will do) draped with large squares of flowered chintz. Smaller conversation tables can be covered in solid tablecloths or in an assortment of chintzes. Mixed patterns have the random charm of a real garden: don't be afraid to mix napkins, china, and silverware too, as long as they all fit into the romantic feeling of your party.

You can't have too many flowers at a garden party, especially when they are presented in loose, casual arrangements. A white wicker basket filled with wildflowers is all the centerpiece your main serving table will need, and baskets of ferns or flowers hanging from trees can dress up the rest of the yard.

PRESENTING THE FOOD: Your cold food will look as pretty and inviting as a garden if you nestle it among fresh greenery. For a delightful basket effect surround plates of CREAM CHEESE PINWHEELS and ALMOND CHICKEN PUFFS with twisted grapevine wreaths. Tuck tiny flowers and ivy leaves into the vines. Watercress-lined silver platters make a nice background for STUFFED SNOW PEAS and HAM ROLL-UPS.

Serve the SHRIMP TAIWAN in an easy-to-prepare cabbage dish. For the shrimp, cut a cabbage head in half, fold back the leaves at the base, and secure the shrimp with toothpicks; for the sauce cut a large center from a second cabbage and set a glass bowl into the cavity. Place both cabbages in a large white basket lined with lettuce leaves, and don't forget a nearby waste bowl for discarded picks.

Raid grandmother's attic for footed cake stands and other old-fashioned dishes to serve ORANGE GLAZED PECANS and PUFF PASTRY STRAWS. A silver chafing dish on your main food table will keep the CRABMEAT DIP warm.

ANOTHER TOUCH:

• A beautiful silver tea service is a nice touch on the serving table, certainly very much in keeping with your English Garden.

English Garden Party
Serves 50 Guests

Timetable	Recipe	# of Recipes	Storage
2 Weeks Ahead	Chicken Almond Puffs	2	F
1 Week Ahead	Orange Glazed Pecans	1½	C
	Citrus Cooler	1½	F
2-3 Days Ahead	Pineapple-Date Dip for Apples — make spread only	2	R
	Shrimp Taiwan — prepare and marinate	3	R
1 Day Ahead	Ham Roll-Ups	2	R
	Avocado Egg Mold with Caviar	1	R
	Velvet Crab — prepare dip except for crab	1	R
Morning of Party	Stuffed Snow Peas	4	R
	Cream Cheese Pinwheels — assemble but do not slice at this time	2	R
Afternoon of Party	Pineapple-Date Dip for Apples — slice apples and soak in lemonade concentrate	2	R
	Puff Pastry Straws — assemble	2	R
	Citrus Cooler — partially thaw and add final ingredient		
Serving Time	Puff Pastry Straws — bake		
	Cream Cheese Pinwheels — slice and bake		
	Pineapple-Date Dip for Apples spread on apples slices		
	Chicken Almond Puffs — bake		
	Shrimp Taiwan — bake		
	Velvet Crab — add crabmeat and heat		
	Pimm's Cup	50	

C = airtight container
F = freezer
R = refrigerator

Almond Chicken Puffs

OLÉ

Sombreros

South of the Border Dip

Mexican Cheesecake

Salsa Cruda   Guacamole

Green Chili Bites

Macaroon Fruit Dip

White Sangria

Mexican and Domestic Beer

**Salsa, Sangria and
Sombreros
Friday, July 27
7:00
Sarah & Robert White
2 Gleneagle Court**

**Regrets:
555-6432**

OLÉ

The cheerful sight of traditional Mexican luminaries lighting your front path and the sound of mariachi music in the air will let your guests know from the very start that they are in for a festive evening. The sights and sounds of a Mexican fiesta lend themselves perfectly to a big backyard party, so indulge yourself: the theme here is fun with a south of the border accent.

DECORATIONS: Think of the colors of Mexico as you plan your decorating scheme: hot pink, yellow, blue, and green, as well as adobe and terra cotta. Cover your serving tables in bright, solid-colored cloths and dress them up with contrasting napkins. Clay serving dishes carry out the Mexican theme (the dish doesn't have to be Mexican — anything from a French earthenware casserole to a well-lined clay flower pot will do!). Colorful paper plates and plasticware are in keeping with the festive, informal atmosphere of this fiesta party.

For a real fiesta touch, don't forget the piñata. Early in the evening the piñata can have place of pride as a centerpiece on your main serving table. For a grand finale hang the piñata over a branch (far away from the table) and let blindfolded guests take a chance at smashing it with a broomstick. Fill the piñata with jellybeans, hard candies, or your favorite after dinner mints.

Carry the Mexican theme to every corner of your yard with lighted torches and more luminaries. Mexican and American flags flying from a flagpole or hanging from the eaves of the house are colorful reminders of your party's theme.

PRESENTING THE FOOD: Use a large earthenware platter for the MEXICAN CHEESECAKE — it's delicious but messy! The MACAROON DIP AND FRUIT, on the other hand, is colorful enough to be part of your table decorations. For a festive presentation, halve a pineapple lengthwise and hollow it out, saving the shell. Place the two halves next to each other at the back of a large lettuce-covered tray. Surround the pineapples with sugared grape clusters. (Immerse the grape clusters in beaten egg white and sprinkle with cinnamon and powdered sugar; place on wax paper). Let the rest of the fruit flow forward toward the front of the tray. Place a small bowl of macaroon fruit dip forward from the center and spear several pieces of fruit with colorful cocktail picks.

OTHER TOUCHES:

• Serve the colorful sangria in clear glass pitchers or punchbowl.

• An old-fashioned iced washtub will keep the beer cold. To reduce sweating on the bottles and to add a festive touch, tie napkins cut from colorful cloth around the necks of the bottles. For authenticity mix some Mexican beer in with the domestic brands.

• Plastic coated wire baskets can be filled with bright shredded tissue paper to add another easy note of color to the table.

OLÉ
Serves 100 Guests

Timetable	Recipe	# of Recipes	Storage
1 Week Ahead	Green Chili Bites — prepare	5	F
2-3 Days Ahead	Salsa Cruda	2	R
1 Day Ahead	Sombreros — prepare shells and filling	8	R
	Macaroon Fruit Dip	2	R
Morning of Party	South of the Border Dip — combine ingredients	2	R
	Mexican Cheesecake	3	R
	White Sangria	6	R
Afternoon of Party	Guacamole	3	R
	Sombreros — assemble		R
	Chill beer		
Serving Time	Green Chili Bites — heat		
	South of the Border Dip — heat		
	Sombreros — bake		

C = airtight container
F = freezer
R = refrigerator

Macaroon Fruit Dip

A Seaside Sunset Party

Shrimp in Fresh Dill Marinade

Buried Crab   Rum Sausages

Marinated Vegetable Medley
Herb Curry Dip

Party Snacks

Barbecued Nuts   Zesty Nibbles

Strawberry Margaritas

Cocktails by the Sea

Saturday, August 16

5 to 7

John and Suzy Decker

#2 Salt Meadow Lane

Figure Eight Island

Regrets: 555-4567

A Seaside Sunset Party

Where the quiet-colored end of evening smiles...
— Robert Browning, "Love Among The Ruins"

The sun setting over the marsh, turning the sky to pink and gold, marks the end of another beach day — the perfect time for a carefree gathering of friends. The accent for your Seaside Sunset Party is quick and easy. As the menu demonstrates, you can be quick and easy without sacrificing the extra touches that turn a gathering of friends into a party to remember.

The menu given here accommodates about 25 guests for cocktails: although the hors d'oeuvres are filling, they are not meant to substitute for dinner. Make it clear on your invitation that the party is from 5 to 7, and, chances are, many of your guests will team up to go out to dinner afterwards.

DECORATIONS: Decorations can be simple and casual. The setting, whether it is a deck overlooking the marsh or a view of the evening tide, is your most powerful asset. Your guests in their colorful summer clothes and glowing tans will brighten the scene.

Let your imagination find new ways of using the things you have to reinforce the theme — beach toys, seashells, hurricane lamps. Kites can add both color and a sense of humor to the party. Use a long-tailed dragon kite as a runner down the serving table, fly another kite over the house to welcome guests, and hang a colorful wind sock from the deck. For extra panache, coordinate awning striped paper napkins with the kites.

PRESENTING THE FOOD: The food for this late-afternoon before-dinner party should be presented in a light and casual way. Serve the SHRIMP IN FRESH DILL MARINADE in sailboats of hollowed zucchinis, with a napkin on a skewer for a sail. The HERB CURRY DIP will look especially festive in a red cabbage "flower". Cut a deep circle into the cabbage head from the center to about two-thirds of the way down; remove the center and make v-shaped cuts from the top to about halfway in and two-thirds of the way down. Peel back the leaves into a flower shape. Place the bowl of dip in the center of the flower.

To make clean-up even easier use disposable glasses, and serve the food with paper napkins instead of plates.

OTHER TOUCHES:

• Large seashells can be pressed into service as food servers. Filled with sand, smaller seashells make handy (and safe) ashtrays.

• Plastic sand buckets and digging tools can do double duty as colorful centerpieces or food containers.

• As the sun goes down citronella candles in glass globes will both light the scene and help to keep away uninvited insect guests.

A Seaside Sunset Party
Serves 25 Guests

Timetable	Recipe	# of Recipes	Storage
2-3 Days Ahead	Barbecued Nuts	1	C
	Zesty Nibbles	1	C
1 Day Ahead	Shrimp in Fresh Dill Marinade	2	R
	Marinated Vegetable Medley	1	R
	Herb Curry Dip	1	R
	Rum Sausages	2	R
Morning of Party	Party Snacks — prepare cheese mix	1½	R
	Buried Crab	1	R
Afternoon of Party	Strawberry Margaritas	6	F
	Party Snacks — spread cheese mix		R
Serving Time	Party Snacks — broil		
	Rum Sausages — heat		

C = airtight container
F = freezer
R = refrigerator

Shrimp in Fresh Dill Marinade

Traveling Gala

Party Ham

Crab Verde   Bull's Eye

Pepper Jelly Mold

Blue Cheese Wafers

Louisiana Dip   Cherry Bombs

Butterless Salted Pecans

Tangy Orange Cheese

Fruit Slush   Whiskey Punch

Please join us for
a Gala Evening
honoring
Out of Our League, Too
Saturday, November eighth
seven o'clock
220 State Street
Junior League of Greensboro

R.S.V.P. 555-8226

A Traveling Gala

Joy, pleasance, revel, and applause . . .
— William Shakespeare, Othello

Every organization is faced sooner or later with the task of mounting an ideal party in a setting with less-than-ideal amenities. The ultimate challenge to your entertaining skills is a cooperative reception for 250 in a location without a kitchen. With creativity and resourcefulness, you can sail through your Traveling Gala with ease.

The key to success for this type of function is volunteers. The planning and execution of a successful party can draw an organization together, but don't overtax your human resources. Make sure that your menu is not time consuming or costly. Remember also that simplicity will insure quality control.

DECORATIONS: Cover an eight-foot table with a white cloth and add a three-inch-wide fabric runner in a color that reflects either your setting or your theme. Evenly space three identical centerpieces along the runner. The centerpieces will be the focal point of the table: a cookbook, a basket of flowers, or the organization's three-dimensional logo. Sprinkle the runner with colorful confetti and attach three helium balloons to each centerpiece with ribbon streamers.

Paper napkins and plates are practical in this pared down setting, but make them special by again using your dominant color theme.

PRESENTING THE FOOD: Simplify, simplify and your affair will go smoothly. In planning your menu always keep in mind how your food will be transported, and how best to present it with minimum strain on your volunteers or facilities.

Here are a few general guidelines that can be applied to many menus:

• A chafing dish is invaluable for heating and serving food, not only is it elegant, but it requires no electricity.

• You can keep food such as ham biscuits, canapés, or cheese wafers warm without a chafing dish if you take the proper precautions. While still at home wrap your food in aluminum foil, heat it to serving temperature, and wrap it in a thick layer of newspaper. Place the bundle in a cooler (styrofoam is the lightest and easiest to transport) on a layer of potholders. Your food will stay hot for several hours, but don't open the cooler more often than you need to. For sauces and dips, follow the same technique, but heat the food in a sturdy casserole. Pack the casserole in newspapers and transport as above.

• Cold items can become soggy from melting ice if they are not packed carefully. When finger sandwiches or bread-based items must be chilled for transport, layer them in a large cardboard box (a shirt or dress box is ideal) between sheets of wax paper. A damp paper towel between the wax paper layers will help to keep the sandwiches fresh. When you are ready to deliver the sandwiches, place the closed box on a foil-covered bed of ice.

• Cold dip travels best in a well-sealed plastic container in a cooler with ice or several ''blue ice'' packs. Cut vegetables at home and store them in zip-locked bags packed in ice.

• When making finger sandwiches ahead of time, spread one side of your bread with non-whipped tub butter to keep the bread from drying out or getting soggy.

DON'T FORGET...

The following emergency kit should travel with you whenever you are faced with a no-kitchen challenge like this one. Plan ahead and save yourself hours of frustration.

Emergency Kit:

Extension cords
Warming trays
Crock pots
Toothpicks
Masking tape
Denatured alcohol
Trash bags
Paper towels in abundance
Butter spreader
Sharp knives

Vegetable peeler
Can opener
   (the old-fashioned hand-held kind)
Slotted spoon
Extra crackers
Parsley
Pre-sliced lemon
Whole lemon and lime
Jug of water
Damp cloths for wiping

A Traveling Gala
Serves 250 Guests

Timetable	Recipe	# of Recipes	Storage
2 Weeks Ahead	Crab Verde	5	F
	Butterless Salted Pecans	3	C
	Blue Cheese Wafers	10	F
1 Week Ahead	Fruit Slush	12	F
2-3 Days Ahead	Pepper Jelly Mold	5	R
	Party Ham	25 lbs.	R
	Louisiana Dip — prepare dip and cut vegetables	4	R
	Tangy Orange Cheese	6	R
Morning of Party	Bull's Eye	5	R
	Cherry Bombs	10	R
	Party Ham — slice		R
Afternoon of Party	Louisiana Dip — arrange vegetables		R
Serving Time	Whiskey Punch	12	

C = airtight container
F = freezer
R = refrigerator

Party Ham

How Much to Prepare for 100 People

When serving 100 guests, remember to prepare two meats, a cheese, a dip or spread, a vegetable or fruit and a sweet. The table will look more balanced with an even number of dishes and without numerous bread trays laden with crackers and chips. The following amounts are merely suggestions, and will vary according to season, time of party and guest list. The estimates are based on amount needed to serve 100 guests for three hours with five to six items on the table and a dessert.

Food	Quantity
Beef Tenderloin, carved	20 lbs
Beef, shaved	10 lbs
Bread, party	10 loaves
Brie	3 lb wheel
Canapés	200
Cheese Block	3 lbs
Cheese Ball	3 balls
Chicken drumettes	300
Chicken Salad	20 lbs
Crackers	6 boxes
Fresh fruit	24 cups
Ham, shaved	10 lbs
Meatballs	250
Molds: cheese, vegetables, seafood	8 cups
Mushrooms, stuffed	200
Sauces for dipping	6 cups
Shrimp	14 lbs, peeled
Sweets	100
Turkey, shaved	10 lbs
Vegetables	12 cups

Index

Appetizers, *Southern Style*
P.O. Box 935
Waycross, Georgia 31502

Please send me_____copies of **Appetizers, *Southern Style*,**
$6.95 each plus $1.25 postage & handling for first book, only 50¢
postage & handling for each additional book. Georgia residents add
6% tax.
Enclosed is my check or money order in the amount of $_____

Name_____

Address_____

City_____State_____Zip_____

- -

Appetizers, *Southern Style*
P.O. Box 935
Waycross, Georgia 31502

Please send me_____copies of **Appetizers, *Southern Style*,**
$6.95 each plus $1.25 postage & handling for first book, only 50¢
postage & handling for each additional book. Georgia residents add
6% tax.
Enclosed is my check or money order in the amount of $_____

Name_____

Address_____

City_____State_____Zip_____

- -

Appetizers, *Southern Style*
P.O. Box 935
Waycross, Georgia 31502

Please send me_____copies of **Appetizers, *Southern Style*,**
$6.95 each plus $1.25 postage & handling for first book, only 50¢
postage & handling for each additional book. Georgia residents add
6% tax.
Enclosed is my check or money order in the amount of $_____

Name_____

Address_____

City_____State_____Zip_____

Please list any bookstores or gift shops in your area that you would like to handle this book.

pepper jelly mold p. 49
sour dough Bread p. 12
rum sauage p. 23 / Pinneapple sauage p. 2

Please list any bookstores or gift shops in your area that you would like to handle this book.

Please list any bookstores or gift shops in your area that you would like to handle this book.